TEN
SUPER SUNDAYS

The Thrilling Story of the Super Bowl

NFL

By Rick Smith

SCHOLASTIC BOOK SERVICES
New York Toronto London Auckland Sydney Tokyo

Cover Photo by Tony Tomsic

Other Photography Credits

Bob Allen, 92; John E. Biever, 76, 106, 110, 114; Vernon J. Biever, 10, 18, 27, 32, 36; David Boss, 14, 68, 80, 84, 118, 122; Chance Brockway, 44; Malcolm Emmons, 22, 48, 52, 56, 64; Tak Makita, 2; Fred Roe, 40, 60; M.V. Rubio, 102; John Walther, 97; Herb Weitman, 72, 88.

Copyright © 1976 by National Football League Properties, Inc. All rights reserved. Published by Scholastic Book Services, a division of Scholastic Magazines, Inc.
National Football League Properties, Inc., 410 Park Avenue, New York, New York, 10022. NFLP Creative Services, 10880 Wilshire Boulevard, Los Angeles, California 90024.

12 11 10 9 8 7 6 5 4 3 2 1   11   6 7 8 9/7 0 1/8

Printed in the U.S.A.   01

Contents

The Vince Lombardi Super Bowl Trophy.

INTRODUCTION
A Game Is Born

Two men approached each other and shook hands in the shadow of a Texas Ranger statue at the Love Field airport in Dallas, April 6, 1966.

Lamar Hunt, president of the Kansas City Chiefs of the American Football League, and Tex Schramm, general manager of the Dallas Cowboys of the National Football League, were meeting to discuss a possible merger between the NFL and the newer American Football League.

They were meeting in secrecy and in such an unlikely place because the leagues were "at war."

The National Football League had been in business since 1920. Over the next 40 years other professional football leagues had been formed to challenge the NFL, but all of them had gone out of business.

The AFL was different. Besides having a few wealthy team owners, the AFL had a multi-million-dollar television contract to televise its games.

Since 1960, the AFL and NFL had waged a costly battle for the country's top college football players. But the cost of fighting this war had taken its toll. Some teams in both leagues were in danger of going out of business.

Two months after Schramm and Hunt first met, the war was over. An exciting peace lay ahead. It had been agreed that the 9 teams in the AFL would join the 15 teams in the NFL. Two more teams—eventually New Orleans in the NFL and Cincinnati in the AFL—would be added later. By 1970, the merger would be complete, with a 26-team NFL.

During the completion of the merger teams from both leagues would play each other in preseason games, beginning in 1967, and in a championship game matching the two league champions, beginning at the end of the 1966 season. That championship game became known as the Super Bowl.

The Super Bowl, played on a Super Sunday each January, is the country's most popular sporting event. More than 80 million television viewers watched the tenth Super Bowl (Super Bowl X) between the Pittsburgh Steelers and Dallas Cowboys in 1976. It was the largest audience ever to watch a television program.

The Columbia Broadcasting System paid the NFL $3.5 million for the right to televise the game in 1976. Advertisers paid CBS as much as $230,000 a minute for television commercials during the game.

Cities throughout the country report that business falls off almost 70 percent during the game. Sheriff's offices and police departments report fewer complaints. City utility departments report large reductions in water pressure when television viewers take a break from the game during halftime and time outs for commercials.

When the first Super Bowl was played in Los Angeles in 1967, only one person was seen on the main business street of Green Bay, Wisconsin, home of the Green Bay Packers, who were playing the Kansas City Chiefs. That person was a policeman on his beat.

During one Super Bowl week in New Orleans, the proprietor of one of the city's leading restaurants reported that business was so good his customers consumed 24,000 oysters.

Thousands of fans flock to the city hosting the Super Bowl each year. Since the third Super Bowl in Miami in 1969, the game has been sold out months in advance. The demand for tickets to Super Bowl XI in the Rose Bowl stadium in Pasadena, California in 1977 exceeded the supply almost as soon as the site for the game was announced. The Rose Bowl seats 105,000 persons.

How did the Super Bowl get its name?

Lamar Hunt blurted out the words "Super Bowl" during a meeting of AFL and NFL owners in 1966. But he said the credit should go to his 8-year-old daughter. Hunt came home one evening with a toy for her. It was a Silly Putty ball. Chasing it around the house one night, the girl told her father it could do amazing things.

"It's my Super Ball," she said.

The little girl had helped make history.

The Chiefs' Willie Mitchell gets a free ride from Max McGee, who caught seven passes for 138 yards, and scored twice.

SUPER BOWL

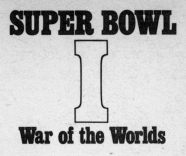

War of the Worlds

The first Super Bowl was a war of the worlds.

The American Football League represented one world and the National Football League represented another.

When the Kansas City Chiefs of the AFL and the Green Bay Packers of the NFL came together in Super Bowl I on January 15, 1967, it was comparable to warriors from distant planets colliding in battle for the first time.

For seven years, from the time the AFL was formed in 1960, the most discussed topic in sports was whether the AFL was equal to the NFL.

There were many fans who expected the Packers to win by a big margin over the Chiefs. But there were plenty of others who felt the Chiefs could defeat the NFL champions. Some sportswriters from NFL cities added fuel to the fire by calling the Chiefs "a Mickey Mouse team from a Mickey Mouse league."

Such differing opinions contributed to the excitement and mystery surrounding the first Super Bowl. The best team in the National

Football League finally was going to play the best team in the American Football League.

The Memorial Coliseum in Los Angeles was the site of the Super Bowl I. More than 1,500 sportswriters and radio and television people from around the country covered the game.

They began gathering in Los Angeles the week after Kansas City had beaten Buffalo 31–7 for the AFL title and Green Bay had beaten Dallas 34–27 for the NFL championship.

The Chiefs flew to Los Angeles 11 days before the Super Bowl. They trained in Long Beach, a city of 350,000 residents 20 miles south of the Coliseum.

The Packers did not come to Los Angeles until a week before the game. They worked out in Santa Barbara, a city of about 70,000 persons 90 miles northwest of Los Angeles.

When the Packers arrived, they were greeted by a barrage of strong words from Fred Williamson, a defensive back for the Chiefs. Williamson became a central figure in the first Super Bowl.

Williamson, who had a talkative reputation in the AFL, called himself "the Hammer." That was how Williamson described the karate-like blow he administered to the helmet of anyone trying to catch a pass in his territory.

"The Hammer ... that's me," said Williamson. "I've broken thirty helmets. I'm going to lay a few hammers on the Packers."

Williamson also insulted Carroll Dale and Boyd Dowler, the Packers' two starting wide receivers. "They don't compare with the good receivers in our league," he said. "After they get hit by the Hammer they'll stagger back to the

12

huddle. They'll tell Bart Starr [the Packers' quarterback], 'Bart, baby, throw to the other side . . . throw to the other side! Stay away from the Hammer!' "

The Packers didn't seem concerned with Williamson's boasts, but they were aware of the challenge posed by the Chiefs.

"The first few days in California were the most tense of the season," said tackle Bob Skoronski. "The guys were edgy. Some of them were downright mean."

No one was more edgy or mean than Vince Lombardi, the Packers' legendary coach. Lombardi, whose disposition usually was like an erupting volcano, pushed and drove his team in practice.

Lombardi knew that if the Packers lost to the Chiefs, they'd never live it down. No one would remember the fact that the Packers had won four NFL championships in six years . . . only that they had been the team to lose the first Super Bowl . . . the NFL team that lost in the first showdown with the AFL.

Lombardi also was concerned with the problem of preparing for an opponent he'd never seen. "If Kansas City had played one team from our league, I could make a judgment," he said. "Studying the films doesn't give an accurate rundown on this team's ability, because I don't know the personnel of that league. Offhand, I'd say Kansas City is a team of many strengths."

Defensive tackle Henry Jordan of the Packers said: "There's been a lot of talk about the NFL being better than the AFL. Mainly this idea has developed because people don't like to change.

Green Bay's Henry Jordan hits Len Dawson's arm and the result was a wobbly pass that Willie Wood intercepted, setting up TD.

"We are older than the AFL, but not better. I look for a good game."

As the Super Bowl drew nearer, it became apparent the rising tension was having more effect on the Chiefs than it was on the Packers.

The Chiefs were upset with Williamson's continual popping off. Head coach Hank Stram told the player to cool it. Ironically, the Packers had decided they would "pick on" Williamson and Willie Mitchell, the Chiefs' starting cornerbacks. The Packers felt they were the weakest links in the Kansas City defense.

When Super Sunday finally arrived, the tension was so intense around the Chiefs that Stram asked some of his players what they thought of his getting a couple Mickey Mouse hats as a gag to ease the players' tightness.

That morning at the Coliseum, the team's trainer and equipment manager had their "ears" on as the athletes came in to have their ankles taped before the game.

Some of the players thought it was childish. Others laughed. But it did get their minds off the game for a moment. That wasn't to say the Chiefs weren't aware of the importance of the Super Bowl. Each player on the winning team would receive $15,000. Each player on the losing team would receive $7,500.

But it was more important than that. League pride was at stake. So were personal reputations.

All of these thoughts were racing through Lombardi's head. He was so nervous during a pregame television interview on the field with Frank Gifford that his hand was shaking and he was perspiring as he answered questions.

The teams also were nervous and cautious once the game began.

Green Bay scored first after almost nine minutes had been played in the first quarter. Starr passed 37 yards to Max McGee for a 7–0 lead. McGee had caught only four passes all season. However, when Dowler was hurt on the game's fourth play, McGee replaced him.

But Kansas City came right back to score. Scrambling out of the passing pocket constantly, Chiefs' quarterback Len Dawson completed several passes to running back Mike Garrett and his two outside receivers, Otis Taylor and Chris Burford.

Dawson got Kansas City's first touchdown on a pass to running back Curtis McClinton. The crowd of 61,946, most of which seemed to be pulling for the Chiefs, cheered the seven-yard score.

After Jim Taylor ran 14 yards for another Green Bay touchdown, the Chiefs replied with a 31-yard field goal by Mike Mercer. That ended the scoring in the first half.

For the first 30 minutes of the game, the NFL's worst fears were confirmed. It actually seemed the Chiefs might win. The Packers' lead was 14–10, but statistically, the Chiefs were ahead. They had 11 first downs to 9 for Green Bay. They had 181 total yards to 164. They had 144 passing yards to 113 and they had 51 rushing yards to 37. Dawson had completed 11 of 15 passes, Starr 8 of 13.

"When we went to the dressing room at halftime, we were confident of victory," said Chiefs' coach Stram.

16

But the Chiefs were emotionally finished at the half. Green Bay was just warming up. The Packers' defensive line had been unable to tackle Dawson in the first half. So they changed their defensive strategy in the second half. The Packers sent their linebackers blitzing into the Chiefs' backfield and Dawson was dropped for losses three times.

On another, critical occasion in the third quarter, Dawson got off a wobbly pass when his arm was hit by tackle Henry Jordan. Willie Wood of Green Bay intercepted the pass and ran 50 yards to the Chiefs' 5-yard line.

Running back Elijah Pitts scored on the next play, following Skoronski's block. That made the score 21–10. Green Bay suddenly was in command.

The Packers scored again late in the third period. Starr's pinpoint passing to McGee was responsible for gains of 11, 16, and 13 yards. The 13-yard completion made the score 28–10.

The Packers scored once more in the fourth quarter. Starting from the 20-yard line, Starr passed 25 yards to Dale. Then he passed 37 yards to McGee. He passed seven yards to Dale to put the ball on the Chiefs' 11. Jim Taylor and Pitts ran the ball in for the touchdown from there, Pitts getting the score from one yard. The margin had reached 35–10. It would be the final score.

The Packers' impressive victory was accomplished by some outstanding third-down performances. Green Bay scored two touchdowns on third-down plays. It maintained ball control throughout the afternoon by converting 10 of 14 third-down plays into first downs. And on

With the Packers in front 28-10, Jim Taylor sets up their last touchdown with tough inside running near the goal line.

their two second-half touchdown drives, the Packers exposed the weakness in the Kansas City secondary. Starr completed passes five times in the area covered by Willie Mitchell.

Starr finished the day with 16 completions in 23 passing attempts for 250 yards and two touchdowns. McGee caught seven passes, three more than he had all year, for 138 yards and two touchdowns.

McGee said the Packers weren't concerned about Williamson's "hammer." "I caught two or three on his side," said McGee. "He lowered the hammer on me one time, but it was more like a tack hammer than a sledge hammer."

Early in the fourth quarter, Williamson was knocked cold when he tried to tackle the Packers' Donny Anderson.

"It was kind of funny," said Gale Gillingham, the guard who was leading Anderson on the play. "Nobody was mad at him. In fact, we thought the things he said were pretty funny. But it was ironic seeing him carried off the field. The fans probably thought, 'Oh, boy, the Packers took care of him.' The Packers didn't get him . . . he got himself."

"I went to make a tackle head first," said Williamson after he recovered. "I caught Anderson's knee on the forehead."

When Lombardi was asked why it took so long for the Packers to "get" Williamson, he smiled. "It took him that long to make a tackle," the coach said.

Lombardi was asked to compare the Chiefs with NFL teams. "In my opinion, the Chiefs don't rate with the top teams in the NFL," he said. "They are a good football team with fine speed, but I'd have to say NFL football is better. Dallas is a better team and so are several others.

"That's what you wanted me to say, wasn't it?" he asked the large crowd of writers and broadcasters. "Now I've said it. But I don't like to get into that kind of comparison."

McGee expressed the same opinion differently: "If there's any doubt now about who's number one, they should let us play Alabama [a top college team] tomorrow and get it over with."

McGee also indicated that the Packers thought the Chiefs "weren't in good shape."

"I resented that more than any other statement," Chiefs' defensive end Jerry Mays said later. "We worked awfully hard; I'm sure as hard as Green Bay, but by halftime we were completely spent.

"I hadn't slept for three nights . . . at least not more than two or three hours a night. I was so nervous that I smoked twice as many cigarettes as I normally do and drank five times as much coffee."

Mays thought for a moment. "The Packers beat us in the first half," he said. "The Packers and the Packers' reputation beat us in the second half. The way I see it, we lost our poise after Wood's interception."

"We had to show clearly just how big a difference there was between the teams," said Packers' defensive end Lionel Aldridge. "I didn't know how bad we'd have to beat them . . . but one touchdown wouldn't have been enough."

Chiefs' running back McClinton and Packers' guard Jerry Kramer said it best for both teams.

"I was overwhelmed by the feeling there would never be another chance," McClinton said later. "I felt there would never be another Super Bowl . . . or another football season.

"Never before had I felt like such a loser. The Packers exposed our weaknesses to the world. They picked apart our defense; they stopped our offense. They demoralized us. There was nothing to indicate the game could have gone either way."

"We've made winning a habit," said Kramer. "It's a matter of pride. We never consider the possibility of losing. This was the Green Bay Packers' fourth championship in six years. That's not easy. That's why the thrill of winning a championship intensifies each time it happens."

KANSAS CITY.....	0	10	0	0	— 10
GREEN BAY......	7	7	14	7	— 35

GB—McGee 37 pass from Starr (Chandler kick)
KC—McClinton 7 pass from Dawson (Mercer kick)
GB—Taylor 14 run (Chandler kick)
KC—FG Mercer 31
GB—Pitts 5 run (Chandler kick)
GB—McGee 13 pass from Starr (Chandler kick)
GB—Pitts 1 run (Chandler kick)
Attendance—61,946

'Packers' coach Vince Lombardi leads the cheers as Green Bay nears
its fifth championship in seven years.

SUPER BOWL

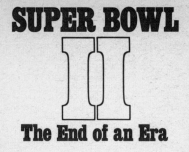

The End of an Era

Vince Lombardi had become a football legend in the 1960s. His gapping, tombstone-sized teeth and cat-that-swallowed-the-mouse smile was as much a part of the Green Bay Packers' tradition as the team's outstanding record since he became coach in 1959.

The mystery of Super Bowl II was not whether the Packers would win (they were heavily favored over the Oakland Raiders), but what the future held for Lombardi.

There had been rumors during the 1967 season that Lombardi, whose teams had won four NFL championships and one Super Bowl in the previous six years, was going to retire from coaching. Vince Lombardi not coaching the Packers? It was a shocking thing for Green Bay players and fans to consider.

"We've heard the rumors," said wide receiver Max McGee, who was coming to the end of his fourteenth season with the Packers and would be playing the final game of his career.

"We've heard the rumors and we know there is

something to them," McGee went on. "It's something you don't like to think about, but you must. I guess all good things must come to an end sometime."

McGee and his teammates had similar feelings about their coach. There were days they hated Lombardi. The coach would drive the team mercilessly in practice and he often would scream at a player for making a mistake. But the Packers loved and respected their coach, too. Lombardi's personality was that strong.

"He can get the best out of more people than anyone I've known," said McGee. "It isn't just Bart Starr or one of the top players. He can get the best out of the fortieth man on the squad. He can get the best out of a secretary in the office ... or our bus driver."

The secret of the Packers' success wasn't just good football players. It was the overpowering influence of Lombardi.

A victory over the Oakland Raiders in Super Bowl II would give Lombardi and the Packers five championships in seven seasons. Most pro football observers felt that Lombardi then would step down and concentrate on his other job as the Packers' general manager.

And there was no doubt among most people that the Packers were going to beat the Raiders. In fact, the often-asked question of which was stronger, the AFL or NFL, had been answered to most people's satisfaction. The Packers had won the first Super Bowl 35-10. NFL teams also had won 27 games against 12 losses and 1 tie in competition with AFL teams in the 1967 pre-season. The AFL's only real moment of glory came when Kansas City beat the Chicago Bears 66–24.

For Green Bay, the hard part was getting to the Super Bowl II. The 1967 season had been difficult for Lombardi and his aging team. The Packers won 12 of 14 regular season games during the year of Super Bowl I. In 1967, their record was 9–4–1, including losses in the last two games of the regular season.

Then the Packers qualified for the Super Bowl by coming up with two of the greatest performances in the team's history. In the first round of the playoffs, they beat the Los Angeles Rams 28–7 two weeks after they had lost to the same team 27–24. They played the Dallas Cowboys the next week for the NFL championship. Trailing 17–14, the Packers' scored the winning touchdown with 13 seconds left in the game. The 21–17 victory was accomplished on one of the coldest days in NFL history. It was 13 degrees below zero when the game began.

The situation in Oakland was just the opposite. The Raiders whipped Houston 40–7 for the AFL title and were a young team on their way up.

Oakland had won only 3 of 28 games in 1961 and 1962, but in 1963 it hired Al Davis as head coach and general manager. Under Davis, the Raiders quickly became one of the top teams in the AFL.

Davis gave up coaching after the 1965 season to run the organization from the front office, but the Raiders' success on the field continued. Their 13–1 record in 1967 was the best in professional football since the Packers were 13–1 in 1962.

But the Raiders did not have the respect that Green Bay had. "We're young and unknown," said Bill Budness, a 24-year-old linebacker. "But we're professionals, too, and we want recognition."

Budness was sitting in his room at the Raiders' Super Bowl training camp in Boca Raton, Florida, a few miles north of Miami. "The Packers are considered to be the best in football, and *if* we beat them . . ." Budness's voice trailed off.

"The Packers and I grew up together," he said. "I never met one of them personally, but it'll be almost like playing our fathers."

While some of the Raiders seemed uncertain about their chances of victory, the Packers were confident. "The difference between our attitude for this game and our attitude for the games with Los Angeles and Dallas was obvious," guard Jerry Kramer said after the game, speaking of the Packers' previous two opponents.

"For those games, Vince didn't have to tell us how good the other team was . . . and we didn't have to convince ourselves. We knew the Rams and Cowboys were tough. But we had to keep saying that about Oakland. We had to force ourselves to respect Oakland."

The Packers were concerned with more important problems. "It wasn't *if* we win, it was *when* we win," said Kramer. One of the Packers' problems was how they would celebrate in the dressing room—especially if this was going to be Lombardi's last game.

"I just can't imagine us throwing coach Lombardi in the shower or pouring something over his head," said tight end Marv Fleming. "You

Donny Anderson ran two yards for a touchdown in the third quarter that increased the Packers' lead to 23-7.

don't do those things to coach Lombardi."

Other Packers' players privately said they were not overly impressed by what they saw of Oakland in the three movies the Raiders provided them for scouting purposes.

The year before, watching Kansas City films, the Packers occasionally had broken into laughter at some Kansas City errors. They did not do it as often watching the Raiders, but once, when two Oakland defensive backs collided and fell down, the Packers laughed out loud.

"I hope we don't get blown out of the ball park," Raiders' coach Johnny Rauch said at one of his press conferences. "We're basically a defensive team . . . our defense can do a great job. But we still have to get points on the board."

The questions Lombardi was asked were about his future. Only once did he hint that his coaching career might be near an end. "I haven't decided," he said in response to a question. "I really have not decided. I do know that in pro football today it is almost impossible to be a coach and a general manager at the same time . . . and to do a good job at both."

After the Packers' final practice session, Lombardi called the team together.

"I want to tell you how very proud I am of all of you," he said. "I have told you before that you are the finest team in all of professional football. It's been a long season, and Sunday may be the last time we are all together. Let's make it a good game, a game we can all be proud of."

No one in the room looked at the coach. If there were tears in Lombardi's eyes, the Packers did not want to see them. They were crying, too.

A capacity crowd of 75,546 persons in the Miami Orange Bowl was on hand in 86-degree weather. This meant that the Packers were playing in temperatures 99 degrees warmer than they experienced two weeks before in Green Bay against Dallas.

It did not bother them, however.

The Packers began slowly but surely. They scored first on Don Chandler's 39-yard goal in the first period. A 20-yard field goal by Chandler increased their lead to 6–0 in the second period.

There were signs of a rout in the making when Starr passed to Boyd Dowler on a play that covered 62 yards and a touchdown in the second period. The 6-foot 5-inch Dowler ran an inside pattern, got past Raiders' cornerback Kent Mc-Cloughan, and was beyond the last defender when he caught the ball.

But Oakland then made its best showing of the day. The Raiders mounted a quick two-minute touchdown drive of 78 yards in nine plays. Four plays were completed passes, two to Bill Miller, who scored on a 23-yard pass from quarterback Daryle Lomonica.

The score was 16–7 at the half, after Chandler's third field goal, a 43-yard kick.

In the second half, the Packers were sharper. "Some of us old heads got together at halftime," said Kramer. "We decided we'd play the last thirty minutes for the old man. We didn't want to let him down."

Green Bay increased its lead to 23–7 on Donny Anderson's two-yard run in the third quarter. Chandler's fourth field goal, from 31 yards, made the score 26–7 in the same period. Cornerback

Herb Adderley picked off one of Lamonica's passes in the fourth quarter and raced 60 yards for the touchdown that made it 33–7.

The Raiders did not score again until almost six minutes had passed in the fourth quarter. Again, Lomonica hit Miller for a 23-yard touchdown pass.

But the Packers' second straight Super Bowl victory already was wrapped up. Kramer and Gregg lifted Lombardi onto their shoulders as the final gun sounded.

"One more time, coach," they said. Lombardi looked at his two all-pro offensive linemen and said, "This is the best way to leave a football field."

A few weeks later, Lombardi announced his retirement from coaching. He turned the head coaching job over to his longtime defensive coach Phil Bengtson but remained as the Packers' general manager.

His self-imposed retirement did not last long, however. After one year the rumors that he would return to coaching became fact. In 1969, Lombardi became head coach and general manager of the Washington Redskins, a team with a long history of little success. The situation was almost identical to that which Lombardi faced his first year in Green Bay.

In 1959, Lombardi had improved the Packers from a 1–10–1 record the year before to 7–5. In 1969, he improved the Redskins from a 5–9 record the year before to 7–5–2.

But Lombardi developed cancer in 1970 and died at 57 a few weeks before the start of the season. The Packers have not returned to the Super Bowl since.

```
GREEN BAY........  3  13  10  7  —  33
OAKLAND.........  0   7   0  7  —  14
```

GB—FG Chandler 39
GB—FG Chandler 20
GB—Dowler 62 pass from Starr (Chandler kick)
Oak—Miller 23 pass from Lamonica (Blanda kick)
GB—FG Chandler 43
GB—Anderson 2 run (Chandler kick)
GB—FG Chandler 31
GB—Adderley 60 interception (Chandler kick)
Oak—Miller 23 pass from Lamonica (Blanda kick)
Attendance—75,546

When Matt Snell scored on a four-yard run in the second quarter, it was the first time an AFL team led in the Super Bowl.

SUPER BOWL

Joe Guarantees It

Joe Namath and his New York Jets' teammate Jim Hudson were standing in a restaurant in Fort Lauderdale, Florida.

A large, rugged-looking man approached.

"I'm Lou Michaels," he said.

Namath nodded at the linebacker of the Baltimore Colts and younger brother of Walt Michaels, an assistant coach with the Jets.

"You're doing a lot of talking," Michaels said.

"There's a lot to talk about," Namath answered. "We're going to kick the stuffing out of your team."

"Haven't you heard of the word modesty, Joseph?" Michaels replied.

Aware that Michaels was getting mad, Hudson suggested to Namath that they go to a table for dinner. But when they sat down, Michaels and his companion, Colts' guard Dan Sullivan, joined them.

"You still here?" Namath needled Michaels.

"Yes," Michaels answered. "I want to hear all you got to say."

"I'm going to pick you apart," said Namath.

"You're going to find it hard throwing out of a well," said Michaels.

"My blockers will give me time," said Namath.

"I never heard our quarterback, Earl Morrall, or any of the great ones, like Johnny Unitas or Bobby Layne, talk like that," said Michaels.

"I believe that," said Namath.

"Even if we get in trouble, we'll send in the master, Unitas," said Michaels.

"I hope you do, because that'll mean the game has gone too far," said Namath.

"Too far what?" snapped Michaels.

At that point, Michaels invited Namath to go outside to the parking lot to settle their argument. Namath, however, excused himself.

While he was gone, Hudson tried to calm Michaels, but Hudson made Michaels even madder when he said, "Your brother, Walt, told our team not to worry about the Colts' kicker coming down the field to make a tackle on a kickoff." Lou Michaels also was the Colts' kicker.

When Namath returned, Michaels was still fuming.

"Suppose we kick *your* pants off," Michaels said. "Just suppose we do that. What then, Namath?"

"I'll tell you what I'll do," said Namath. "I'll sit in the middle of the field and cry."

They all laughed and the tension eased. A while later, Namath paid for dinner with a $100 bill and drove Michaels and Sullivan back to their hotel.

Super Bowl III was Joe Namath's Super Bowl. From the moment the New York Jets arrived in Fort Lauderdale to begin preparing for the game against the Colts in Miami's Orange Bowl, Namath was the center of one controversy after another.

The cocky young quarterback described Earl Morrall, the Colts' starting quarterback and the NFL's most valuable player in 1968, as not being as good as five or six quarterbacks in the AFL. He went so far as to suggest that Morrall would be the number three quarterback on the Jets, behind Namath and Babe Parilli.

A threat was made on Namath's life in New York, and FBI agents checked the Galt Ocean Mile Hotel in Fort Lauderdale to make sure no one could take a shot at him in his hotel room.

Namath missed a Jets' picture day session with press photographers when he overslept. Jets' coach Weeb Ewbank fined him $50.

Namath taunted the Colts in the newspapers . . . the *super* Colts, who were being called the greatest team in NFL history.

The super Colts, who had won 13 of 14 league games, who had beaten the Cleveland Browns 34–0 for the NFL championship, who were favored by as much as 19 points to beat the Jets and hand the AFL its third straight one-sided loss in the Super Bowl.

A group of 55 writers covering the game predicted the score of the game. Forty-nine chose the Colts. A Chicago reporter said they would win 55–0. A man from Baltimore predicted a 48–0 victory.

Amid all of the favoritism of the Colts, Namath kept hammering away. He said the Colts' "great" defense could be beaten. He said

In one of the game's biggest plays, Jim Hudson of the Jets intercepts pass for Jerry Hill near the end of the first half.

the Jets would establish a running game, something no NFL team was able to do consistently against Baltimore. Namath said the Jets' running game would create opportunities for his team to pass.

Namath said the game would be a challenge for the Jets, but that it also would be a challenge for the Colts.

The Colts couldn't believe what they were reading and hearing.

"How does Namath get off criticizing Morrall?" demanded Baltimore coach Don Shula. "Morrall's done a job for us, coming in when Unitas got hurt. Namath hasn't faced the defenses Morrall has."

"Joe's young," said Billy Ray Smith, a defensive tackle for Baltimore. "Some day he'll get a little humility."

"Namath shouldn't talk like that," said Colts' defensive end Bubba Smith. "A professional doesn't say things like that."

But Namath hadn't finished talking. He had hardly begun. Three days before the Jets were scheduled to play the Colts, the Jets hosted a barbeque dinner for their players and wives. Namath appeared only long enough to eat a plate of food and chat briefly with some of his teammates.

Then he left for the annual Miami Touchdown Club dinner. Namath was going to receive an award from AFL commissioner Milt Woodard after being named the outstanding professional football player of the 1968 season.

About two hours later, Namath stepped to the microphone in a Miami Springs hotel. "This isn't an award for me," he began. "Had it not been for my parents and my family, and my high school coach, Larry Bruno, and my college coach at Alabama, Paul Bryant, and many other people— including all my teammates—I wouldn't be here. This should be a most valuable player award for the entire team. You can be the greatest athlete in the entire world, but if you don't win those football games, it doesn't mean anything.

"And we're going to win Sunday, I'll guarantee you."

I'll guarantee you. Namath *guaranteed* the Jets would win. The Jets, who won the AFL championship by a 27-23 score over an Oakland team that had been beaten soundly by Green Bay in Super Bowl II.

The Jets were underdogs by almost three touchdowns, but Namath was having none of that. The reaction from the audience was quick.

"Siddown!" someone hollered.

"That must be a guy from Baltimore," Namath barked back. "Maybe Lou Michaels. Well, those are my feelings, and I'm entitled to them, just as reporters are entitled to theirs."

The next day reporters surrounded many of the Jets and Colts and asked for their reaction. "I don't think any ball player should start in a game or even show up if he doesn't think his team has an opportunity to win," said Jets' coach Ewbank.

What about him *guaranteeing* you'll win?

"That's the way he feels about it," said Ewbank, "and I'm for him. I don't think Joe's trying to con anyone at all."

The father of George Sauer, a Jets' pass

catcher, felt differently. "This is really going to stir up the Colts," said George Sauer, Sr., the Jets' director of player personnel.

"When all this talk started I felt the same way," said Jets' defensive end Gerry Philbin. "But now I'm beginning to think it's good. One of the troubles with the other two AFL teams in the Super Bowl was that most of the players kept saying how great the Packers were . . . so as not to get the Packers mad. But the trouble was, the AFL players began to believe it themselves."

"He's given our players more incentive," Shula said. "Our football team is conscious of what goes on, what is being written. Joe has made it much more interesting."

Norm Van Brocklin, a former champion quarterback in the NFL, was asked what he thought. "I'll tell you what I think of Namath Sunday night," said Van Brocklin. "After he's played his first pro game."

But there was one important NFL official who realized that there was truth to what Namath was saying. "Will the Colts win easily?" a newspaperman asked Vince Lombardi, the former coach of the Packers.

"You know where my heart is," answered Vince. "But don't be surprised if this isn't a runaway. The Jets are capable of giving them a great fight."

You mean Namath?

"He's very dangerous and he has receivers who can catch the ball."

There were 75,389 persons in the Miami Orange Bowl when the Jets took the opening kickoff. On the first play, Namath sent fullback

Joe Namath counts the seconds as the game nears an end, while Jets' coach Weeb Ewbank (next to Namath) keeps eyes on field.

Matt Snell into the right side of the Colts' line for three yards. On the second play Namath sent Snell into the same hole.

Snell, a former All-America from Ohio State, had played six seasons in the AFL. He also had been drafted by the New York Giants of the NFL. The Giants said Snell signed with the Jets because he didn't think he was good enough to play in the NFL.

Snell quietly steamed at such suggestions. He was furious when writers covering this game said he and his backfield running mate Emerson Boozer were not as good as the Colts' runners, Tom Matte and Jerry Hill.

Snell had something to prove. He was as dedicated to winning this game as any man on the field.

After Snell took the ball from Namath, he blasted into the Colts' defense and, creating an opening, headed for the outside and up the sideline. Colts' defensive back Rick Volk came up to make the tackle after Snell had gained nine yards.

But when the players unpiled to return to the huddle, Volk remained on the ground. He had been knocked unconscious when he hit Snell. Namath had established the Jets' running game.

The Jets broke a scoreless deadlock in the second quarter on the same kind of play. Snell ran four yards for a touchdown and the AFL was ahead for the first time in the Super Bowl.

Field goals of 32, 30, and 9 yards by Jim Turner gave the Jets a 16–0 lead in the fourth quarter.

The Colts replaced Morrall at quarterback, sending Johnny Unitas into the game when the score was 13–0 with almost four minutes left in the third quarter. Morrall had not seen wide-open receiver Jimmy Orr in the end zone near the end of the first half. He threw to Jerry Hill instead, and Jim Hudson intercepted.

Unitas directed the Colts on an 80-yard touchdown march in the fourth quarter to narrow the score to 16–7. But the Jets never were in real danger. The final 16–7 score was more indicative of the difference between the teams than the statistics.

The Jets had 337 total yards to the Colts' 324 and 21 first downs to 18, but no one doubted New York was the best team on the field. All because of a young quarterback who completed 17 of 29 passes for 206 yards and sent Matt Snell into the Colts' line 30 times for a record-setting 121 rushing yards and one touchdown.

Jets' coach Ewbank had been fired as head coach of the Colts in 1963. His replacement was the present Colts' coach, Don Shula. Ewbank could have gloated over the Jets' victory. But when Ewbank and Shula met in the center of the stadium at the end of the game, the New York coach said, "We had all the breaks."

"Your team played well," Shula said.

Quickly, they parted, but Shula, reflecting later on Ewbank's graciousness, said, "I thought that was pretty nice of him to say that."

Shula was just as gracious in the losers' dressing room. "Namath was all we had heard," he said. "He's a fine football player.

"The story of the game was simple," said Shula. "We didn't do it and they did. We had plenty of opportunities, especially in the first half. We didn't make the big plays we have all season. We dropped some passes. We just didn't do it. They deserved it."

Then Shula considered the long winter and spring that faced the Colts. "We'll have to be men enough to take this," he said.

Namath meanwhile was refusing to talk to writers from NFL cities. But he soon changed his mind. "If you guys had seen us play during the season, you wouldn't have been surprised," he said.

The Jets voted Namath the game ball. He promptly announced he would give it to the AFL.

And Jets' kicker Jim Turner said, "Hello, world. Welcome to the American Football League."

N.Y. JETS............	0	7	6	3 —	16
BALTIMORE..........	0	0	0	7 —	7

NY—Snell 4 run (Turner kick)
NY—FG Turner 32
NY—FG Turner 30
NY—FG Turner 9
BALT—Hill 1 run (Michaels kick)
Attendance—75,389

The Chiefs' Otis Taylor gets ready to straight-arm Minnesota's Karl Kassulke as Kansas City breaks open the game.

SUPER BOWL

The Chiefs' Revenge

The week before the Super Bowl had been the most miserable of Len Dawson's life.

It began with a nationally televised report that his name had been linked to a federal gambling investigation in Detroit. Dawson was innocent of any wrongdoing, but he had been under intense pressure for several days.

If that weren't enough to ruin his concentration for the upcoming game, Dawson greeted Super Sunday with an upset stomach that kept him awake the night before.

At breakfast that morning, Dawson managed to get down some crackers and milk, but he gave up on the orange juice after a few sips. In a few hours, the 34-year-old quarterback and his Kansas City Chiefs would play the Minnesota Vikings in Super Bowl IV at Tulane Stadium in New Orleans, Louisiana.

The Chiefs were the first AFL team to make a repeat trip to the Super Bowl. But most of the experts said Kansas City's prospects for victory were not much better than when the Chiefs lost to the Green Bay Packers 35–10 in Super Bowl I.

For the fourth successive year, the NFL champion was a big favorite to defeat the AFL champion. The Vikings, who had been formed only eight years before, won 12 of 14 regular season games in 1969 en route to their first NFL championship.

Minnesota had run roughshod over the NFL with two big weapons: A feared defensive line known as the "Purple People Eaters," and Joe Kapp, a big, powerful quarterback who liked to run as well as pass.

Kapp joined the Vikings in 1967 after eight years in the Canadian Football League. He quickly became one of the most popular and respected players in the NFL. The Vikings' slogan, "40 for 60," had been coined by Kapp when he refused to accept the team's most valuable player award at the end of the regular season.

"There ain't no red-nosed reindeer; there ain't no Santa Claus, and there ain't no most valuable Viking," said Kapp. "It was forty for sixty." Kapp meant the honor should go to all 40 Minnesota players who had gone all out for victory in 60 minutes of every game.

Kapp's stature also was increased when the Vikings beat the Cleveland Browns 27–7 for the NFL championship. Early in the game he ran into and over Jim Houston, Cleveland's 240-pound linebacker, knocking Houston out of the game. Kapp proved he was as tough as he was talented.

Neither Dawson nor the Chiefs were supposed to have those qualities. Dawson was completing his thirteenth professional season. But NFL people were quick to point out that his first five seasons were with NFL teams and he was unable to win a starting job.

The Chiefs did not even win their division championship in 1969. They finished second to Oakland in the AFL's Western Division. But the AFL postseason format in 1969 allowed a second-place team to go to the playoffs.

The Chiefs beat the New York Jets 13-6 in the first round of the playoffs, then defeated Oakland 17-7 for the championship.

As Dawson looked around the team's hotel dining room on the morning of Super Bowl IV, he noticed that, like himself, few teammates had eaten their breakfasts.

The quarterback then glanced at his watch and decided to return to his room. In a little more than an hour, buses would leave to take the team to the stadium.

Dawson's roommate, Johnny Robinson, was waiting for him with a friend, who had worn Robinson's black blazer with the Chiefs' red emblem on the lapel pocket when the Chiefs beat the Jets and Raiders the previous two weeks.

When the man inquired about the blazer, Robinson said the coat was with his wife, who was staying at another hotel. The friend insisted on wearing the coat.

Robinson's wife could not be reached, however. She had gone to church. Dawson then called his wife, Jackie, and instructed her to ask the hotel bell captain to open Mrs. Robinson's room.

Dawson's wife picked up the blazer and paid a cab driver $20 to deliver it to the Chiefs' hotel. "I

Kansas City quarterback Len Dawson had plenty of time to throw. He completed 12 of 17 passes for 142 yards and a touchdown.

never saw more superstitious people," said Dawson.

When the Chiefs boarded their buses, the police escorts who were supposed to lead them to Tulane Stadium were nowhere to be seen. All week, when they didn't need an escort, there had been one.

The Chiefs left for the stadium, anyway, but when they arrived they had difficulty getting to the assigned parking area.

Head coach Hank Stram explained to a security officer that this was the Kansas City football team . . . it was going to play the Minnesota Vikings that afternoon . . . and could the bus be driven to the entrance to the dressing room as the driver had been instructed?

Not getting anywhere, Stram finally told the driver, "Go on through. Don't worry about him. We have to get to the ball park."

As they began putting on their uniforms, the Chiefs saw something different. The 1969 season had been the NFL's fiftieth. All NFL teams, including the Vikings in the Super Bowl, wore shoulder patches on their uniforms in recognition of the fiftieth season.

For the Super Bowl, the Chiefs had shoulder patches on their uniforms in honor of the AFL's tenth and final season. The merger with the NFL would be complete in 1970 and the AFL no longer would exist.

When Dawson finished putting on his uniform, he and Stram began going over the Chiefs' game plan. The biggest concern was the Vikings' front four. Minnesota's ends, Carl Eller and Jim Marshall, were so fast the Chiefs did not feel they could run conventional end sweeps. And the pass rush of Eller, Marshall, Alan Page, and Gary Larsen was so quick at penetrating into the opponent's backfield that Dawson probably would not have time to wait for a receiver to get open on a long pass pattern.

"We had to run straight at them and throw short passes in front of their cornerbacks," said Dawson.

The Chiefs also decided to put two linemen over the Vikings' center. They hoped to keep Kapp in the passing pocket, preventing him from running with ball.

It could have been a game plan made in heaven, as far as the Chiefs were concerned. Just about everything they tried was successful.

The first team to score had won the first three Super Bowls—and Kansas City scored first against the Vikings when Jan Stenerud kicked a 48-yard field goal in the first quarter.

Stenerud added another, from 32 yards, early in the second quarter, and another, from 25 yards, in the second quarter.

The Chiefs well-planned strategy was evident in the drive that led to Stenerud's third three-point kick.

They surprised the Vikings by springing wide receiver Frank Pitts on an old-fashioned end-around play. Pitts circled back from the line of scrimmage, took a handoff from Dawson, and ran 19 yards to set up the score.

The fourth time the Chiefs scored they went into the end zone for a touchdown. Mike Garrett ran five yards through the left side of the line. The score was a shocking 16–0 at halftime.

"Thirty more minutes and we're world champions," Stram told the Chiefs before they returned for the third quarter. "Play control ball and don't make any mistakes."

Minnesota was in control at the start of the second half, however. The Vikings managed a 69-yard scoring drive that ended with Dave Osborn running four yards for a touchdown.

"Let's put out that fire," Stram told Dawson. "Let's not let them get any closer."

There were nearly 20 minutes left in the game and the Chiefs were worried. Dawson began moving them upfield, but in five plays they had advanced only from their 18-yard line to the 32. It was third down and seven yards for a first down.

Once again, Dawson called for Pitts to run the end-around. And for the third time, it worked. Pitts gained seven yards and a first down. Pitts gained 37 yards in the three times he was asked to run against the Vikings, who had not seen the play in the three game films they received from the Chiefs.

Dawson overthrew Pitts on the next play, but the Vikings were penalized 15 yards for a personal foul. Now the ball was on Minnesota's 46.

Dawson then threw a short pass to Otis Taylor in front of Earsell Mackbee, the Vikings' cornerback. Mackbee suffered a pinched nerve in his neck on the play as he attempted to tackle Taylor, who broke free and raced down the sideline. The last man with a chance to catch Taylor was Karl Kassulke.

Taylor gave Kassulke a fake and a straight-arm and Kassulke fell down at the 10-yard line.

51

The Chiefs led 23-7 in the fourth quarter when Willie Lanier intercepted Joe Kapp's pass and returned it nine yards.

Legs pumping high, Taylor strutted into the end zone for a touchdown.

The score was 23–7. Part of the third quarter and all of the fourth quarter remained. But the Vikings were beaten.

Not long after the touchdown, the Chiefs' Aaron Brown made certain of a Vikings' collapse. Brown tackled Kapp for a loss, hitting Kapp with such force the quarterback had to leave the game with an injured shoulder.

"The Kansas City defensive line looked like a redwood forest," Kapp said later, referring to Brown and Buck Buchanan, both of whom stood 6 feet 7 inches.

It had been three years since the Chiefs' loss to the Packers in Super Bowl I, but the memory still was bitter. Garrett, appearing on national television after the game, said, "Just want to say I remember what Vince Lombardi said three years ago about us; that we're not as good as a lot of NFL teams. Love ya, Vince."

Defensive end Jerry Mays remembered a humiliating incident late in Super Bowl I. Mays had said before the game that his boyhood idol was Packers' tackle Forrest Gregg. Both players attended Southern Methodist University in Dallas, Texas, and Mays even wore the same number as Gregg: 75.

With the Packers well in front and in possession of the ball in the fourth quarter, Gregg and guard Jerry Kramer came to the line of scrimmage. "Kramer said to Forrest, 'I'll get number fifty-eight, Forrest . . . you take old idol over there,' " Mays recalled.

Lombardi's lack of respect for the Chiefs still

was evident two nights before Super Bowl IV. At commissioner Pete Rozelle's pregame party, the ex-Packers' coach voiced doubt that Dawson and the Chiefs could put together an offense that would keep Page from blowing up the middle and into their backfield.

"I don't think their offense has changed much," said Lombardi, referring to the Chiefs' offense in Super Bowl I. "Besides, they have the same quarterback."

So no one was more pleased than Dawson, who overcame the pressures that beset him earlier in the week and showed the NFL that he was a championship quarterback.

There was one other person who might have been happier: Dawson's son. "I got up on the platform for the television interview and looked down," said Dawson. "There was Lennie, my nine-year-old boy. He had somehow managed to get into the dressing room.

"At that moment, I didn't care about anything or anybody in that entire room except him. He is rather shy, and when I spotted him he didn't know what to do," said Dawson.

"He just looked up at me and said, 'Dad, you done good.' He looked so lost with all the people jostling around him.

"I said, 'Come on up here, Lennie, with me.'" It was one of the father and son's proudest moments.

"For a father, the greatest thing in the world is when his son really looks up to him with admiration and respect," said Dawson. "My son at that particular time was really happy and, I think, proud to be my son. He stood there with my arm around him and said nothing, but I knew he was feeling plenty good."

When Dawson returned to his locker, he summed up the Chiefs' victory.

"The best thing about this game is that we won't have to answer for it the next three years, like we did last time. This time," said Dawson, "we're the champions."

In the clubhouse of the Vikings, the team that had expected to be champions, the only sound in Joe Kapp's corner was the hissing sound of escaping air.

Bob Lee, a reserve quarterback, was letting the air out of footballs to make it easier to ship them home to Minnesota.

"All that work, and this is the way it ends," said Lee.

The deflation of footballs seemed the final act for the Vikings.

They had been punctured by the Chiefs.

```
MINNESOTA.........  0   0  7  0  —   7
KANSAS CITY.......  3  13  7  0  —  23
KC—FG Stenerud 48
KC—FG Stenerud 32
KC—FG Stenerud 25
KC—Garrett 5 run (Stenerud kick)
Minn—Osborn 4 run (Cox kick)
KC—Taylor 46 pass from Dawson (Stenerud kick)
Attendance—80,562
```

Jim O'Brien follows through with the kick that resulted in the field goal that won Super Bowl V for Baltimore.

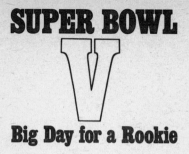

SUPER BOWL V

Big Day for a Rookie

Jim O'Brien of the Baltimore Colts watched the clock tick away . . . 25 seconds . . . 20 . . . 15 . . . 10. Finally, with nine seconds remaining, quarterback Earl Morrall called time.

Baltimore and the Dallas Cowboys were tied 13–13. The 79,204 spectators in the Miami Orange Bowl tensed for the ultimate moment in the game's final seconds.

Morrall returned to the field after a conversation with Colts' coach Don McCafferty. The Colts went into their huddle, then broke and moved to the line of scrimmage.

Kneeling on one knee, Morrall called out the signals. Center Tom Goode snapped the ball. The quarterback placed it on the artificial turf. O'Brien swung his right leg.

The ball went up, end over end. It curved toward the right goal post . . . but then veered back toward the middle and went through. Five seconds remained.

Referee Norm Schachter raised his arms to indicate that O'Brien's 32-yard field goal attempt was good. Baltimore had won Super Bowl V 16–13.

O'Brien leaped in the air and raced toward his teammates on the sideline. His kick had just earned each of them $15,000. It was the dramatic end to an incredible season for the rookie placekicker . . . a great ending to a long year.

The Colts chose O'Brien in the third round of the 1970 NFL draft of college players the previous January. In 1969, O'Brien had set a national collegiate record by averaging 22 yards a catch as a wide receiver for the University of Cincinnati. He also had won seven games at Cincinnati with field goals.

The Colts even had a scout watching O'Brien the day Cincinnati played Miami of Ohio in the team's big game of the year. O'Brien kicked a 47-yard field goal in the final seconds for a 23–21 victory.

Everything went well for O'Brien when he reported to the Colts' training camp in the summer. His competition for the kicking job was Lou Michaels, a 13-year NFL veteran who had played the last six seasons with the Colts.

Michaels and O'Brien waged a spirited battle, but O'Brien won. Michaels was released after the fifth game of the preseason. The Colts decided to keep O'Brien because he was younger and could play two positions. Michaels had played linebacker during his career, but his future did not have the promise of O'Brien's.

That's when the youngster's problems began. Veteran Colts' players viewed the release of Michaels with mixed feelings. Michaels was popular. O'Brien was a rookie . . . and an unusual one, at that. Because of his long hair, many of the veterans called him "Lassie." They also called him a hippie and other not-so-complimentary names.

Worst of all, O'Brien missed two field goal attempts and kicked off poorly three times in a 17–14 loss to Washington in the final preseason game—a week after Michaels had been let go.

The following week the Colts prepared to open the regular season against the Chargers in San Diego. "It looks as if we're going to have to place a call to Swoyersville," said veteran defensive tackle Billy Ray Smith. Lou Michaels lived in Swoyersville, a small town in Pennsylvania.

"I don't blame the vets," O'Brien said. "Michaels was kicking better than me and I was nothing more than a rookie with long hair. Lou was their friend. But I don't think I took a job away from him. I got it because of my youth and the fact I could play two positions."

Early in the game with San Diego, O'Brien missed a fairly easy field goal. That was the difference in the score as Baltimore entered the final minute of play trailing 14–13.

But with 56 seconds left, O'Brien kicked a 28-yard field goal, his third of the game in four tries, and the Colts were able to give new head coach McCafferty a 16–14 victory in his first game.

Afterward, several players congratulated O'Brien in the dressing room. "But I'm going to cut all that hair off before the season's over," promised Billy Ray Smith, who preferred short hair cuts.

"I guess they think I'm kind of a weirdo," said O'Brien. "When they call me a hippie, they're

Dallas's Mel Renfro and Cornell Greene (34) argue with officials over deflected touchdown pass to Colts' John Mackey.

not entirely wrong. I've got some strange ideas."

"He's typical of the kids coming out of college today," said Colts' tackle Dan Sullivan. "He don't give a darn about anybody or anything."

But the Colts came to like and respect O'Brien. He finished fourth in the NFL during the regular season with 93 points and made an important contribution to their success.

The Colts had a record of 11 wins, 2 losses, and 1 tie and won the Eastern Division championship in the American Football Conference. Then they beat Cincinnati and Oakland in the playoffs to gain the Super Bowl.

Baltimore, Cleveland, and Pittsburgh of the NFL had joined the 10 American Football League teams to form the AFC in 1970. This gave both the AFC and the NFC 13 teams, the result of the merger between the AFL and NFL.

The Colts' victory over Oakland in the AFC championship meant that two original NFL teams were meeting in the Super Bowl. The intense feeling of rivalry between the AFC and NFC wasn't as apparent during Super Bowl week as it had been in previous years between the AFL and NFL.

NFL commissioner Pete Rozelle made note of this situation during his pregame press conference. "It has taken something away from the game in my mind," he said, "just as I'm sure it has in other persons' minds but this has been more than made up for by the stature of the game. We never have had this pressure for a ticket to the game the week of the Super Bowl. When we played the game in Miami two years ago, we were not sold out until game time."

That was the Super Bowl in which the heavily favored Colts were surprised and beaten by the New York Jets.

"No one knows how bad we felt," said Colts' linebacker Mike Curtis about the loss to the Jets. The Colts didn't plan to let it happen again, even if the Cowboys were slight favorites to win.

The Colts even went so far as to avoid repeating many of the things they did in getting ready for Super Bowl III. When they flew south to Miami from Baltimore, the Colts went on a different airline. Their headquarters was at the Miami Lakes Country Club instead of the Statler-Hilton Hotel. They practiced at a different site—Biscayne College, instead of St. Andrew's School in Boca Raton.

Colts' defensive end Bubba Smith had another superstition. "In the 1966 Rose Bowl, the Michigan State team I played on was a twenty-point favorite over UCLA and we lost," said Smith.

"In Super Bowl III, we were nineteen-point favorites over the Jets and we lost. Each time we followed the opponent's bus into the stadium. That won't happen again."

A lot of unusual things happened in the first 59 minutes, 51 seconds of Super Bowl V. Maybe it was the pressure of the game. Whatever, the Colts and Cowboys made one error after another. There were 11 turnovers, 14 penalties, and numerous other mistakes. The Colts led in turnovers 7–4, the Cowboys in penalties 9–5.

Field goals of 14 and 30 yards by Mike Clark gave Dallas a 6–0 lead in the first quarter. The Colts drew even in the second quarter in the weirdest of the game's many weird plays.

Quarterback Johnny Unitas threw a pass to Eddie Hinton. But Hinton tipped the ball to Mel Renfro of Dallas. Renfro *also* tipped the ball, and the Colts' John Mackey finally caught it on the Cowboys' 45 and went all the way to complete a 75-yard touchdown play.

The Cowboys argued with game officials that Renfro hadn't touched the ball . . . that the play should have been called back, since two offensive players illegally touched the forward pass. (A television replay showed Renfro's outstretched fingers touching the ball.)

O'Brien then was a participant in one of the Colts' early mistakes. His point-after-touchdown attempt was blocked by Mark Washington when Tom Nowatzke failed to pick up the charging defender. That left the score 6–6.

The Colts weren't through making mistakes, however. Midway through the second quarter, Unitas fumbled and Dallas recovered on the Colts' 28-yard line.

Running back Duane Thomas ran four yards on the first play. Craig Morton passed 17 yards to Dan Reeves, putting the ball on the 7-yard line. Morton then threw a short pass to Thomas, who ran the ball in for a touchdown.

Dallas held on to its 13–6 lead until the fourth quarter, but in between some strange events took place. After Dallas took the lead in the second quarter, Unitas was hurt and replaced by Earl Morrall, whom Unitas had replaced when the Colts were losing to the Jets in the third quarter of Super Bowl III.

Morrall threw a 26-yard pass to Hinton on his first play. Then he hit Roy Jefferson for a 21-

Duane Thomas, whose running sparked Dallas in its drive to the Super Bowl, scored a touchdown to tie the score in second period.

yard gain. Just like that, the Colts were on the Cowboys' 2-yard line. But the Colts did not gain a yard on the next three plays.

There were 21 seconds left in the half. Baltimore called time. A successful field goal by O'Brien would have narrowed the score to 13–9. But instead of an eight-yard field goal, the Colts took a chance and went for a touchdown.

They came up empty when Morrall's pass to tight end Tom Mitchell was incomplete.

Dallas also missed a chance to increase its lead to 20–6 at the start of the third period. Baltimore's Jim Duncan had fumbled the kickoff and Richmond Flowers recovered at the Colts' 31.

In five plays the Cowboys moved to the Colts' 1-yard line, but Duane Thomas fumbled on the 6 . . . and Jim Duncan recovered.

The Colts tied the game again in the fourth quarter after a pass by Morton was tipped by Duncan and intercepted by Rick Volk, Duncan's teammate. Volk returned the ball 30 yards to the Cowboys' 3-yard line. Tom Nowatzke scored two plays later and O'Brien's kick made the score 13–13 with seven minutes, 35 seconds left.

Dallas appeared on its way to victory with three minutes remaining when Ron Widby punted to the Colts' 5-yard line and the Colts couldn't move and had to punt.

With almost two minutes on the clock, the Cowboys had the ball on their own 48 and were in good position to move into field goal range and win. But on one second-down play they lost 24 yards when Morton was tackled for a nine-yard loss and a Cowboys' lineman was penalized 15 yards for holding.

On the next play, Morton's pass was intercepted by Curtis, who ran 13 yards to Dallas's 28. Two running plays by Norm Bulaich advanced the ball three yards. Now it was O'Brien's turn.

O'Brien went onto the field with 32 seconds left. After Morrall called the time out with nine seconds remaining, Dallas signaled it wanted another time out.

"We expected that," O'Brien said later. "In fact, all season, whenever we practiced field goals, Billy Ray Smith would holler, 'Time out! Time out!' just to get me ready for something like this. I thought, 'This isn't anything but Billy Ray Smith.' "

Referee Schachter spared O'Brien a longer wait by ruling the Cowboys could not call time out. According to NFL rules, two consecutive time outs cannot be called without a play being run.

Still, O'Brien was nervous. "The wind?" he whispered to Morrall. "The wind?"

"Wind? There is no wind," said Morrall. "Just kick the ball straight. . . ."

And then it was all over, and O'Brien was making his victory leap.

"It's funny," O'Brien said, smiling amid the bedlam of the dressing room. "I had a dream about this last week. I dreamed of this long field goal going through to end it all . . . but I didn't know who would be doing the kicking. Me or Mike Clark.

"Another funny thing," he said. "My mom called me and said we couldn't lose. She's big on astrology and she figured it all out. I believe in astrology, too. I was born February 2, 1947. This is the age of Aquarius, isn't it? I'm an Aquarius."

"Hey, rookie," hollered Fred Miller, a leader in the Colts' defense. "I just took a survey. You can keep your long hair."

```
BALTIMORE........ 0   6   0   10  —  16
DALLAS............3  10   0    0  —  13
DAL—FG Clark 14
Dal—FG Clark 30
Balt—Mackey 75 pass from Unitas (kick
blocked)
Dal—Thomas 7 pass from Morton (Clark kick)
Balt—Nowatzke 2 run (O'Brien kick)
Balt—FG O'Brien 32
Attendance—79,204
```

Roger Staubach was the most valuable player. He passed for 119 yards and two scores and directed Dallas's big ground attack.

SUPER BOWL

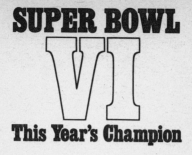

This Year's Champion

The Dallas Cowboys were always called "Next Year's Champions." Next year the Cowboys would win the championship. *Next* year.

The trouble was, it seemed next year never would arrive.

The Cowboys carried the label of losers, but it was not because they always lost. Nothing could have been further from the truth. From 1966 through 1971, Dallas's regular season record was 63 wins, 19 losses, and 2 ties.

But during that time the Cowboys never won the big game, the game people remembered. For example:

In 1966, the Cowboys won the NFL's Eastern Conference championship with a 10–3–1 record. It was considered a crowning achievement in professional football, because the team had been formed only seven years before in 1960.

The Cowboys played the Green Bay Packers for the NFL title and the right to meet the AFL champion in Super Bowl I. But Green Bay won 34–27. Dallas's chances of victory faded away when the Cowboys failed to score after gaining a first down on the Packers' 2-yard line with almost two minutes remaining in the game.

The Cowboys and the Packers met again for the NFL title the following year. Dallas led 17-14 until the final 13 seconds, when Packers' quarterback Bart Starr scored a touchdown for a 21-17 Green Bay victory.

In 1968, the Cowboys won their division championship with a 12-2 record, but they were beaten 31-20 by Cleveland in the first round of the NFL playoffs . . . after having defeated the Browns 28-7 during the regular season.

The Cowboys won their division title again in 1969, winning 11, losing 2, and tying 1 . . . but again they were beaten by Cleveland, 38-14 in the first round of the playoffs.

In 1970 Dallas seemed ready to shed its image as the team that was unable to win the big game. The Cowboys rebounded from a 38-0 loss to St. Louis that dropped their record to 5-4 in the regular season and won their next seven games to gain the right to represent the NFC against Baltimore in Super Bowl V.

But the favored Cowboys saw the Colts score 10 points in the fourth quarter and come from behind to win 16-13 on Jim O'Brien's field goal with five seconds left to play.

But the Cowboys never quit trying. Here they were again, preparing to meet the Miami Dolphins in Super Bowl VI in New Orleans's Tulane Stadium.

They had dominated their competition in 1971. They breezed to a division title with an 11-3 record and defeated Minnesota 20-12 and San

Francisco 14–3 in the playoffs.

They were favored to beat the young, up-and-coming Dolphins. But the question remained: Would this be the game in which the Cowboys became *this* year's champions or would they lose the big game again?

The Dolphins were determined to see that Dallas would lose. And they had a very important person in their corner, the President of the United States.

Not long after the Dolphins beat the Baltimore Colts 21–0 for the AFC championship, then President Nixon placed a telephone call to Dolphins' coach Don Shula. Shula was at his home watching a replay of the Baltimore game at about 1:30 A.M. when the President called. They chatted about 10 minutes.

"When the phone rang at that hour, I thought it might be some nut calling," said Shula. "But somebody said, 'Is this Mister Shula?' Then he said, 'The President is calling.' Everybody in the house was asking, 'Who is it?' I said, 'The President,' but I thought it might be a hoax. I was listening to make sure it was his voice."

Shula said Nixon told him: "Now you understand that I'm a Washington Redskins' fan, but I'm a part-time resident of Miami [the Winter White House was in nearby Key Biscayne] and I've been following the Dolphins real close."

"The President alerted me that the Cowboys were a real good football team. But he told me, 'I still think you can hit Warfield on that down-and-in pass pattern against them.'"

Paul Warfield, the Dolphins smooth, swift wide receiver, caught a long pass from quarter-

The Cowboys' double-team coverage effectively neutralized Bob Griese's pass attempts to dangerous Paul Warfield (top, middle).

back Bob Griese on a down-and-in pattern for a 50-yard gain that set up Miami's final touchdown against Baltimore.

On a down-and-in pattern the receiver usually races straight downfield and veers toward the center of the field.

The Cowboys felt the key to their success on offense was their ability to block the Dolphins' quick middle linebacker, Nick Buoniconti.

"We want to run the ball," said Landry. "If we're going to do that we're going to have to get someone to block Buoniconti.

"They have many young, developing players on defense, but Buoniconti is a real veteran, the key to their defense. We have to make certain on every play that we block Buoniconti."

The Cowboys' running attack was led by Duane Thomas, who had become known throughout the country in 1971 for his refusal to talk to newspaper reporters and most of his teammates and coaches.

Thomas was upset with the Cowboys because of a dispute involving his contract, but this did not stop him from playing a big role in the team's march to the Super Bowl. Thomas ran for more than 800 yards and scored 13 touchdowns.

Shula hoped his inexperienced defense would be able to stop Thomas and the Cowboys' other runners. It was partly because of this and partly because so many of the players did not have big reputations that the Miami unit was called the "No Name Defense."

But it quickly became apparent that the Dolphins were not ready to challenge the Cowboys. The Cowboys won Super Bowl VI 24–3.

The 21-point margin of difference was the second largest in a Super Bowl, four points fewer than Green Bay's 35–10 win over Kansas City in Super Bowl I.

Dallas made only one mistake on offense and defense all through the sunny, 39-degree afternoon. That was when Calvin Hill fumbled on Miami's 1-yard line late in the game. Miami was guilty of two fumbles and one pass interception and mistakes led to 10 of the Cowboys' points.

Duane Thomas ran for 95 yards and one touchdown and Walt Garrison ran for 74 yards as Dallas gained a total of 252 yards on the ground, a Super Bowl record.

The Cowboys ran 69 offensive plays to Miami's 44. They outgained the Dolphins 352 yards total to 185.

There never was much doubt about the outcome to the 81,035 spectators. Even President Nixon's play didn't help the Dolphins.

On Miami's eighth offensive play of the game, Warfield ran a down-and-in pattern. But Cowboys' cornerback Mel Renfro and strong safety Cornell Green had Warfield covered. The pass from Griese was high. Warfield leaped, but the defense did not let him have a chance.

"We made sure they didn't complete that pass on us," said Landry.

"They had two weeks to prepare," said Warfield. "In the films we'd seen of the Cowboys, Green normally moved up to help out against a run. This left an open area downfield. Not so for us. When Green saw me split out to the left, he backed up and turned in toward me." Dallas had taken a 3–0 lead before the play involving Warfield. Mike Clark kicked a nine-yard field goal, which followed a fumble by the Dolphins' Larry Csonka. Chuck Howley had recovered for Dallas at the Cowboys' 48-yard line.

On the play after the incomplete pass to Warfield, Griese dropped back to pass again but was chased out of the pocket by Cowboys' defenders. The quarterback kept backpedaling until Lilly surrounded him and trapped Griese for a 29-yard loss.

Dallas went ahead 10-0 in the second quarter on a seven-yard pass from quarterback Roger Staubach to Lance Alworth. Miami's only score came with four seconds remaining in the half when Garo Yepremian kicked a 31-yard field goal.

The second half also belonged to Dallas. Thomas ran three yards for a touchdown that made the score 17-3 in the third quarter and Staubach threw a seven-yard pass to Mike Ditka to make the score 24-3 in the fourth quarter.

"We took the second-half kickoff and went right down and scored," said Staubach, the game's most valuable player. "That just about finished them off."

"My biggest disappointment was that we never challenged," said Shula. "They completely dominated."

Shula was studying the official statistics of the game. "They had the ball more than forty minutes," he pointed out, "and we had it for less than twenty. That's what happens when one team dominates another."

Offensively, the Cowboys did what they hoped to do. The blocking of guards John Niland,

Duane Thomas eludes Miami Dolphins' pursuers. Thomas led Dallas runners with 95 yards and scored one touchdown.

Blaine Nye, and center Dave Manders opened the holes for Thomas, Garrison, and Calvin Hill. More important, Niland and Manders blocked Buoniconti.

Buoniconti did not know how well. He played most of the second half in a daze. At one point in the fourth quarter he came to the sideline and wondered, "Is the score still ten to three?"

"I got hit in the head, I guess," said Buoniconti after the game. "I'm not sure when it happened. It was in the first half."

"The Dolphins were too young to win it," said Dallas linebacker Dave Edwards. "Their youth kept them from doing a lot of things. They did certain things on certain plays. It was too late in the season for them to make a change. We knew pretty much what they were going to do."

One of the most impressive records set by a Cowboys' player was by Herb Adderley, who was playing in his fourth Super Bowl. The veteran cornerback also set a record by being on the winning team for the third time—twice with Green Bay and once with Dallas. Adderley also played in Super Bowl V for Dallas against Baltimore.

The victory brought Adderley's earnings in the four Super Bowls to $52,500.

The mood in the Cowboys' dressing room was such that even Duane Thomas ended his self-imposed silence.

"Are you happy, Duane?" Thomas was asked.

"Who said I was sad?" Thomas replied.

"Your face doesn't show happiness," someone said.

"Happiness," Thomas said softly, tapping his

chest, "is inside."

No one was happier than Landry or Lilly. Landry had been the Cowboys' head coach since they were organized in 1960. Lilly, around whom Landry built what became Dallas's "Doomsday Defense," joined them in 1961.

Landry was smiling when he accepted a telephone call from President Nixon, who praised the Cowboys for their great effort.

Then Landry smiled again and told how he had received a telegram before the game from an important Cowboys' fan who lived near Austin, Texas—former President Lyndon Johnson.

"My prayers and my presence will be with you in New Orleans, although I don't plan to send in any plays," Johnson's telegram said.

Lilly lit a victory cigar. "I normally don't smoke," he said, "but one of the guys had some of these lying around. I puffed on one during half-time of the first playoff game. We won. I thought it might have been good luck.

"There has been some self doubt on this team," said Lilly. "There has to be when you end a season like we did five years in a row. "We *hadn't* won the big game. It was like a brand."

Lilly said the Cowboys were determined to end their habit of losing the big game. "I can't explain how intense the feeling was. It probably helped us, being that intense. That and the doubt. Now the load is off our shoulders."

Cowboys' general manager Tex Schramm went a step further.

"This is just the beginning," he said. "We have a young team. I can see the Cowboys becoming a dynasty, as the New York Yankees were in baseball. We have many championships in front of us."

Miami's Bob Griese also made a prediction. "We'll be back," he said. "I don't think you can judge a team by one game, especially when a club such as ours has won so many the last couple seasons."

History was to prove Griese right.

```
DALLAS.............  3  7  7  7  —  24
MIAMI...............  0  3  0  0  —   3
Dal—FG Clark 9
Dal—Alworth 7 pass from Staubach (Clark
kick)
Mia—FG Yepremian 31
Dal—D. Thomas 3 run (Clark kick)
Dal—Ditka 7 pass from Staubach (Clark kick)
Attendance—81,035
```

Miami's Manny Fernandez stops the Redskins' Larry Brown and led a defense that shut out Washington's offense.

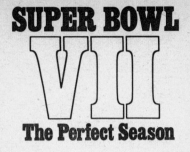

SUPER BOWL VII

The Perfect Season

Loser.

The label haunted the Dallas Cowboys before Super Bowl VI, and it followed Miami Dolphins' coach Don Shula in Super Bowl VII.

It didn't seem to matter that the Dolphins had won 16 straight games in 1972.

It didn't seem to matter that no team in the NFL's 53-year history had ever matched the Dolphins' feat.

It didn't seem to matter that the Dolphins had not lost since their Super Bowl VI defeat to the Cowboys.

What seemed to matter was the fact that since Shula had become a head coach in the NFL in 1963, his teams had not won a pro football championship.

In 1964, Shula's Baltimore Colts were favored over the Cleveland Browns in the NFL championship . . . but lost 27-0.

In 1965, Shula's Colts were eliminated in sudden death in a conference championship playoff by the Green Bay Packers.

In 1967, Shula's Colts, undefeated in 13 games, were beaten 34–10 by the Los Angeles Rams for the NFL's Coastal Division title.

In 1968, Shula's Colts were heavily favored over the New York Jets in Super Bowl III . . . but lost 16–7.

In 1970, Shula's Dolphins were beaten in the first round of the AFC playoffs by Oakland.

In 1972, Shula's Dolphins were the victims of one of the most one-sided defeats in the history of the Super Bowl in game VI against the Cowboys.

People forgot that Shula's record in 10 years as a head coach was 113 victories against only 35 losses, and 5 ties.

They forgot that Shula had won more games in his first 10 seasons than any coach in NFL history.

They forgot that Shula was one of only nine coaches in the NFL whose teams had won at least 100 games.

People remembered that Don Shula was the only coach to lose two games in the Super Bowl.

So it was no surprise that the Washington Redskins were slight favorites to whip the Dolphins in Super Bowl VII. Besides, the Redskins had a history of toppling unbeaten teams.

The 1942 Chicago Bears were the last previous NFL team to win all its regular season games. But the Bears lost the championship game to the Redskins.

Washington won 11 of 14 games in 1972 and defeated Dallas's defending Super Bowl champion for the NFC East title. Then the Redskins beat the Cowboys again 26–3 for the NFC cham-

pionship. The Cowboys had gotten into the playoffs with the best second-place record in the
NFC, enabling them to become the NFC's playoff "wild-card" team.

Washington was known as the "Over The
Hill" gang. Its top players generally were much
older than the average NFL athlete. Coach
George Allen preferred older players.

After leaving the Los Angeles Rams to join the
Redskins in 1971, Allen obtained many of his
former Rams' players in trades. Sometimes the
Redskins were referred to as the "Ramskins."

But they weren't too old and they certainly
weren't over the hill. In 1971, the Redskins made
the playoffs for the first time since 1945; 12 of the
team's 15 previous seasons had been losing ones.

Allen made numerous trades and overhauled
the organization.

Allen was a demon for detail. And he hated
distractions. An example of both took place
before Super Bowl VII.

The game was going to be played in the Los
Angeles Coliseum for the first time since the
Super Bowl began in 1967. Allen's Rams' teams
used to play their home games in the Coliseum.

But to make sure nothing had changed, Allen
had one of his assistants go to the Coliseum and
chart how the angle of the sun would slant into
the eyes of the Redskins' pass receivers and kick
returners.

When it came to distractions, Allen had his fill
during Super Bowl week. He had to agree to
interviews each day with the newspaper, radio,
and television reporters covering the game.

What bothered Allen the most, however, was

Larry Csonka, 235 pounds, was a symbol of strength, speed, and grace as he gained 112 yards in 15 carries.

seeing Tim Foley, a defensive back for the Dolphins, interviewing Redskins' players before the game.

Foley, who was out of the Super Bowl because of an injury, was serving as a reporter for a Miami newspaper. "Heck," said Allen, "he was interviewing me before I realized who he was. I could have told him something that could have helped the Dolphins."

Allen also played a "psyching" game with the Dolphins. He was trying to gain a psychological edge for his team with some of his pregame remarks.

"Since we can't play the game in Washington, I can't think of a place I'd rather play than Los Angeles," he said.

Allen was trying to create a homefield advantage for the Redskins out of a neutral field. "The Dolphins are the best team we have faced in my coaching career," said Allen.

Since one of his teams played against the 1966 Green Bay Packers, considered by many to be the best of all time, Allen was giving the Dolphins the added burden of trying to live up to that praise.

Shula, however, played the psyching game, too. When a reporter asked him what he would do if it rained on Super Sunday and the field was muddy, Shula replied: "Allen has made the statement that he never has lost in the rain. So if it rains on Sunday, we're going to forfeit the game."

But Dolphins' defensive tackle Manny Fernandez said the psyching game was over-rated. "All coaches tell their players not to say anything that will get the other team mad. I don't read what the other team says. I haven't read a newspaper here all week."

Shula, however, was aware of what had been written and said about the fact that his teams had not won the big game. "I can't walk down the street without people coming up to me and asking, 'What happened in the Super Bowl III loss to the Jets?' It's mental torture."

But Shula said he and the Dolphins had learned a positive lesson from their loss to Dallas in Super Bowl VI. "The experience last year was the big thing," he said. "That and the naked realism after it's all over that there is only one winner. That's hard to realize. All week before the game you're treated as equals.

"But as soon as the Super Bowl is over, there's only one team people are talking about. You're thrown back with the other twenty-five teams in the league . . . a loser like the rest of them."

The Dolphins had almost the same team in Super Bowl VII as they had in Super Bowl VI. The big difference, as Shula pointed out, was experience.

There was a question about the Dolphins' quarterback situation, however. Bob Griese, the Dolphins' regular quarterback since 1967, suffered an ankle injury in the fifth game of the 1972 season. His replacement, 38-year-old Earl Morrall, led the Dolphins to 11 straight victories. Morrall was released by Baltimore and picked up by Miami for the $100 waiver price following the 1971 season.

But Griese had played in the second half of the AFC championship victory over Pittsburgh.

Shula decided to start Griese against the Redskins.

The coach made the right decision. It didn't take long for the crowd of 90,182 persons on Super Sunday to see that.

The temperature in Los Angeles was an unseasonably warm 84 degrees, the warmest since Green Bay and Oakland played in 86-degree weather in Super Bowl II. But the Dolphins were even warmer.

After some early experimenting, the Dolphins got down to business the third time they had the ball. Runs of three and eight yards by Jim Kiick set up a 14-yard pass from Griese to Paul Warfield. Larry Csonka then picked up two on the ground and Kiick added four.

Griese then passed 28 yards to Howard Twilley for a touchdown. The Dolphins had marched 63 yards in six snappy plays, scoring with one second remaining in the first quarter.

The Dolphins scored again on a 47-yard pass play involving Griese and Warfield, but the Dolphins' Marlin Briscoe moved forward before the snap of the ball and the play was called back.

This didn't stop Miami, however. Nick Buoniconti, the Dolphins' middle linebacker, picked off a pass thrown by Washington's Billy Kilmer.

Buoniconti returned the ball 36 yards to the Redskins' 27 and five plays later Kiick scored from the 1 with 21 seconds remaining in the half. Only two minutes remained when the Dolphins' drive started, but Griese calmly called two running plays before he threw a 19-yard pass to Jim Mandich on the big play of the drive.

The Redskins were shaken by the turn of

The Redskins' Mike Bass scored on a 49-yard run after a blocked fourth quarter field goal attempt and a fumble by Garo Yepremian.

events. Instead of trailing 7–0 at the half, they were two touchdowns behind.

Washington came back with two long marches in the second half, but both bids ended in frustration. The first drive ended when Curt Knight missed a 32-yard field goal. The second ended when Jake Scott intercepted a pass by Kilmer in the end zone.

The Redskins' offense never scored. It remained for the Redskins' defense to score their team's only touchdown . . . and that was the result of an error by Miami placekicker Garo Yepremian.

With a little more than two minutes left, Yepremian was attempting a 42-yard field goal that would have given Miami a 17–0 lead and put the game out of reach.

Center Howard Kindig made a low snap of the ball, however. This forced Morrall, the holder, to position the ball quickly for the kick. "Garo hit it good, but the ball didn't get up into the air fast enough," said Morrall.

Bill Brundige blocked the kick. Yepremian, a 5-foot 8-inch, 150-pound soccer-style kicker who never had played football in his life and had been only a placekicker in his five-year NFL career, picked up the ball and started running.

Yepremian then tried to throw a pass, but the ball slipped off his hand. Yepremian attempted to regain control of the ball, but he knocked it into the air. Mike Bass intercepted and ran 49 yards for a touchdown with 2:07 remaining in the game.

There was time for Washington to score again, but the Dolphins maintained possession until

1:14 remained.

The Redskins could not rally in the final minute. The game ended with Miami a 14-7 winner.

"This is the first time the goat of the game is in the winners' locker room," said Yepremian. "I should have fallen on the ball. But my mind went blank."

Csonka, whose fumble helped the Dallas Cowboys get started in their rout of the Dolphins the year before, ran for 112 yards in only 15 carries and continually punished the Redskins with his 235-pound strength and speed.

"I know what the Redskins are doing right now," said Csonka. "They're over there in their dressing room figuring out how they're going to win this game next year."

Csonka pointed out that the Dolphins were the fourth team in the last four years to win the second time it went to the Super Bowl. Kansas City had done it in 1970, Baltimore in 1971, Dallas in 1972, and now Miami.

"We never were really in the game . . . and we never were really out of it," said the Redskins' defensive captain, Jack Pardee. "But we'll be back next year."

"The pressure's off," said Shula. "Sure, I was aware of the reputation I'd gotten. The losses in the two Super Bowls were there. No way I could hide them.

"The Super Bowl against the Jets was a great disappointment. I felt we could have busted it open in the first half and scored four touchdowns. But we didn't.

"Last year's Dallas game left me with an

empty feeling. We never challenged. We never played well. I was empty. But all of that is in the past now. That's something I can forget."

```
MIAMI. . . . . . . . . . . . . . .   7   7   0   0   —   14
WASHINGTON. . . . . . . .   0   0   0   7   —    7
Mia—Twilley 28 pass from Griese (Yepremian
kick)
Mia—Kiick 1 run (Yepremian kick)
Wash—Bass 49 fumble recovery (Knight kick)
Attendance—90,182
```

Minnesota could not stop Miami's Larry Csonka. He set rushing records with 145 yards in 33 carries, and scored twice.

SUPER BOWL

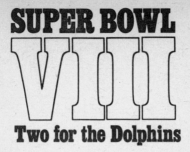

VIII

Two for the Dolphins

The Miami Dolphins led Minnesota 17–0 and had the ball on the Vikings' 2-yard line in the third quarter of Super Bowl VIII.

On second down, quarterback Bob Griese led the Dolphins from their huddle to the line of scrimmage. As he began to crouch behind center Jim Langer, Griese hesitated. He turned his head and asked running back Larry Csonka, "Say, what the heck is the count?"

Griese had forgotten the signal on which Langer was supposed to snap the ball.

"What's the count?" he asked Csonka again.

"Ah . . . it's on two, isn't it?" Csonka replied.

Jim Kiick, the Dolphins' other running back, was listening. "No, no . . . it's on one," he said.

Guard Larry Little heard the conversation and became edgy. "What's it on . . . what's it on?" he demanded.

Langer had not heard the voices behind him and he thought Little was acting strangely.

Griese glared at Csonka and Kiick. Finally, the quarterback decided that Csonka was right. He prepared to take the ball from Langer on a count of two.

Langer knew the count was one, however. He snapped the ball into the palms of Griese's hands on one . . . to the surprise of Griese.

The quarterback juggled the ball and handed off to Csonka, who followed Kiick, Langer, Little, and tackle Norm Evans through the Vikings' defensive line and into the end zone for a touchdown.

That gave Miami a whopping 24–0 lead. For the Dolphins, the job was getting easier each year they played in the Super Bowl. The 71,882 persons at Rice Stadium in Houston, Texas, heartily agreed.

The Dolphins laughed about the incident in the dressing room following their 24–7 victory. "I wound up confusing everyone on the play," said Csonka, who did little else wrong. He set Super Bowl records with 33 carries and 145 yards gained, and scored two touchdowns.

"Bob seemed to bobble the ball a little when he got the snap," said Csonka. "He had that wide-eyed look when he handed me the ball. I'm just happy I didn't cause him to drop the ball."

"When you have a lead like that at that time in the ball game, you like to take a little more time," said Griese. "You either take a long time calling the signals or look over the defenses or something. "In this case, I was looking over their defense to see what I could call on the next play if that play didn't work. Then I forgot the count. I should have known that Csonka was the wrong guy to ask. He was always missing the count back in training camp."

"The hole was there anyway," said Csonka. "Thank the linemen for that. As always, they reacted to the snap of the ball, and I just followed them into the end zone."

The Dolphins had rebounded from a loss to the Dallas Cowboys in Super Bowl VI to become the second team in history to win back-to-back Super Bowls. Their victory in Super Bowls VII and VIII equaled the Green Bay Packers' achievements in Super Bowls I and II.

No team could match the Dolphins' record of appearing in three straight Super Bowls and no man could match Don Shula's record of coaching in four Super Bowls.

Most of the suspense in Super Bowl VIII lasted about five and a half minutes. That's how long it took the Dolphins to accept the opening kickoff and march 62 yards in 10 plays for a touchdown.

"I knew we were in trouble after their first drive," said Vikings' coach Bud Grant. "They didn't do anything we didn't expect. They ran the plays we saw in the movies and they blocked well. They did the things that got them here."

The interesting part of the Dolphins' offense was their "misdirection" plays. As Grant said, the Vikings knew what to expect, but they didn't seem to be able to do anything about it.

The Dolphins scored their first touchdown on a misdirection play. With a first down on the Minnesota 5-yard line, Griese called a play in which the Dolphins' two guards, Little and Bob Kuechenberg, pulled to their right as if the play were going to be a sweep around end.

The Vikings' defensive line, "reading" the

movement of Little and Kuechenberg, took off in the same direction.

Griese then handed the ball to Csonka, who ran through the hole created on the left side by defensive tackle Gary Larsen, who was chasing Little and Kuechenberg.

That's misdirection.

It was typical of how the Dolphins beat the Vikings on a foggy, 50-degree afternoon. Minnesota took the kickoff following the Dolphins' touchdown, but the Vikings had to punt after three plays.

Again, the Dolphins scored in five and a half minutes, moving 56 yards in 10 plays with Kiick going over from the 1-yard line.

After 13 minutes and 38 seconds of play in the first quarter, the Dolphins had run or passed 20 times for 120 yards and had scored 14 points. In the same length of time, Minnesota had run the ball twice and passed it once for a total of nine yards.

Minnesota did not gain a first down until the last play of the first quarter. The Vikings did not move past the 50-yard line until less than three minutes remained in the half. At this point they trailed 17–0, following a 28-yard field goal by Garo Yepremian.

The Vikings got all the way to Miami's 6-yard line a minute before the halftime intermission. But on fourth down and a yard to go for a first down, Oscar Reed fumbled when he was tackled by Nick Buoniconti, and Miami's Jake Scott recovered.

Any hope that Vikings were ready to make a move ended in the third quarter. Minnesota's

Defensive coach Bill Arnsparger (left) and head coach Don Shula of Miami embrace after Dolphins' second consecutive Super Bowl victory.

John Gilliam ran 65 yards with the second-half kickoff, but a clipping penalty by teammate Stu Voigt brought the ball back to the Vikings' 11-yard line.

Three plays later Minnesota was on its 7 and had to punt. Miami took the ball and went 43 yards in eight plays to go ahead 24–0. The touchdown came on the play on which Griese forgot the snap count.

With the 235-pound Csonka around to carry the ball, the Dolphins didn't feel the need to pass. Griese threw only seven times all day, completing six.

But he made good use of the pass. When Miami was driving to the 24–0 lead, the Dolphins faced a third-and-five at Minnesota's 38. For the first time all afternoon, Minnesota's defense was stiffening.

But Griese broke the Vikings' back with a 27-yard pass completion to Paul Warfield that put the ball on the 11-yard line. Five plays later Csonka scored.

Minnesota's only touchdown came at the start of the fourth quarter, when quarterback Fran Tarkenton ran four yards to complete a 10-play, 57-yard drive that began near the end of the third quarter.

The Vikings did not make a real threat again. They got to the Dolphins' 32-yard line, but Curtis Johnson intercepted a pass by Tarkenton. Miami then controlled the ball for the final six minutes and 24 seconds.

Miami's victory came as no surprise. In fact, the Dolphins were the first AFC team to be favored in the history of the Super Bowl.

Since its loss to Dallas in Super Bowl VI, the Dolphins had won 32 of 34 games. They were being compared to the legendary Green Bay Packers' teams.

Tight end Marv Fleming of Miami played on the two Green Bay Super Bowl champions and on the two Dolphins' winners. He had earned approximately $140,000 in money won in playoff games with Green Bay and Miami.

"Vince Lombardi," he said of the Packers' coach, "and Don Shula, my coach here, are the same types. Each is a disciplinarian. Each demands a lot. The difference is that Shula is more friendly.

"You can walk up to Shula after practice and say, 'Coach, can I see you a minute?' He'll stop and talk to you. With Lombardi, you had to have an appointment."

Fleming didn't make a comparison between the teams, however. But Larry Csonka did. "I think we're better than the Packers, but I'm prejudiced," he said, smiling. "I think we have more good players and I think we have a better passing attack than the Packers did."

Csonka was asked how he felt about becoming a part of the Dolphins' legend. "I never really thought about that," he said. "Football is a 'now' thing. It's nice to be on top. But believe it or not, I play football because I like to play football. I don't care much for statistics or who is a legend."

Dolphins' defensive tackle Manny Fernandez spoke along the same lines as Csonka. "I don't worry about whether we're better than the Packers were," he said. "The important thing to me was whether we were better than the Vikings . . .

and we were."

The Vikings, who played in the same division with the Packers, had some interesting thoughts about the Dolphins. "We looked at them on film, and they were the most impressive offensive team we'd seen," said assistant coach Jack Patera. "But we thought some of those teams they played in the playoffs, like Cincinnati and Oakland, didn't prepare for them properly. We took great pains to prepare properly for this game. But they went out and did the same thing to us."

Miami defeated Cincinnati 34–16 in the first round of the playoffs, then stopped Oakland 27–10 for the AFC championship.

When the Dolphins arrived at their training camp during Super Bowl week, they acted as if the big game was just another game. "Jim Kiick and I were talking about that," said Csonka. "The first couple years in the Super Bowl were different. First, there's the idea of being in it. The next year it was coming back and proving we weren't as bad as we looked the year before. I'm not saying I'm bored with it or the team is bored with it. The game is still exciting and it's great to get the chance to prove you're the best team in professional football. But it's not as exciting as it was the first time."

Dolphins' coach Don Shula did not agree. He called the Super Bowl VIII victory "a greater accomplishment" than winning all 17 games and Super Bowl VII the year before.

"This year," he said, "everyone was after us. We were the champs. They were taking their best shots at us. We met the challenge."

No one could deny that.

```
MINNESOTA.........    0   0   0   7  —   7
MIAMI..............   14   3   7   0  —  24
```
Mia—Csonka 5 run (Yepremian kick)
Mia—Kiick 1 run (Yepremian kick)
Mia—FG Yepremian 28
Mia—Csonka 2 run (Yepremian kick)
Minn—Tarkenton 4 run (Cox kick)
Attendance—71,882

Franco Harris scored the Steelers' first touchdown and set Super Bowl records with 34 carries and 158 yards gained.

SUPER BOWL
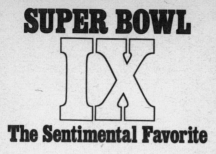
The Sentimental Favorite

The Pittsburgh Steelers were posing for a team picture at Tulane Stadium in New Orleans before Super Bowl IX when center Ray Mansfield was gripped by a haunting memory.

In a few days the Steelers would meet the Minnesota Vikings with the opportunity to win the first NFL championship in the 43-year history of the franchise. But Mansfield wasn't thinking about that. His thoughts were on the final game of the 1969 season, Chuck Noll's first season as the Steelers' head coach . . . the year the Steelers won their first game and lost the next 13.

"Our thirteenth loss was in this same stadium," Mansfield said later. "We had reached the low point in Steelers' history in this stadium . . . and here we were five years later playing in the Super Bowl in the high point in Steelers' history."

Mansfield had been with the Steelers since 1964. Until Noll became the coach, it appeared that he was certain to spend his entire career with a losing team.

But it took awhile for Noll to build the Steelers. From that 1–13 start, the Steelers improved to 5–8–1 in 1970 and inched their way to 6–8 in 1971. Then they turned it on with an 11–3 record that won the AFC Central Division title in 1972.

The Steelers beat the Oakland Raiders in the first round of the playoffs that year but lost to Miami in the AFC championship. They were 10–4 in 1973 and were eliminated in the first round of the postseason games 33–14 by Oakland.

Most experts agreed the Steelers of 1973 had an outstanding defense and a number of top offensive players . . . but they were lacking a solid quarterback.

Terry Bradshaw was expected to be the quarterback who would lead the Steelers to a championship. He was their number one pick and the first player chosen in the NFL's 1970 college draft.

But Bradshaw's play was uneven during his first four seasons and in the 1974 preseason he lost his job to Joe Gilliam. Gilliam started well, leading the Steelers to a 30–0 victory over Baltimore in the regular season opener. But Gilliam's play was uneven, too. After the sixth game, Bradshaw became the starter again. But four games later, Terry Hanratty started.

It was obvious the Steelers weren't going to the Super Bowl until their quarterback situation was straightened out. The problem created so much discussion around Pittsburgh that one of the city's major newspapers ran a poll.

"Pick Your Quarterback," the newspaper asked its readers.

Bradshaw received twice as many votes as Gilliam and Hanratty, and, as luck would have it, Noll picked him to start the next week.

The Steelers beat New Orleans in that game but lost to Houston the following week. In the thirteenth game of the season, they went to New England to play the high-scoring Patriots.

"I don't know what it was but Bradshaw was a changed man that day," said Mansfield.

New England got off to a 7–0 lead in the first quarter. Bradshaw quickly was tackled for losses of 13 and 2 yards trying to pass, and he was mad.

"Terry came into the huddle the next time we got the ball and you could tell he was really angry," said Mansfield. "It sparked us. We took the ball and dominated the rest of the game. It was the offense that picked up the Steelers that day. Bradshaw and the offense.

"At the start of the game, Jim Plunkett and New England moved the ball on our defense as if it wasn't there . . . and we had depended on our defense so much the last three years. We always felt, 'Let the defense do it.'

"When the offense started moving, the defense picked up. From that point, we destroyed everyone."

Coming into the Super Bowl, the Steelers had won four games in a row and had gotten better each week. They whipped New England 21–17 and Cincinnati 27–13 to end the regular season. They beat Buffalo 32–14 in the first round of the playoffs. They stopped Oakland 24–13 in the AFC championship and held the Raiders to 29 yards on the ground.

Bradshaw played brilliantly during the string

The Vikings raise their hands to signal touchdown by Terry Brown (24) after Matt Blair blocked punt by Bobby Walden.

of victories, but when he arrived at the Steelers' Super Bowl training camp he was surrounded by unimpressed reporters.

The question on almost all of their minds was about Bradshaw's IQ. He had a great passing arm, they admitted, but they didn't think he was very smart.

"I'm smart enough," Bradshaw said. "You don't have to be an Einstein to play this game. It's unfortunate, but I've found that once you've been labeled in pro football, there's not much you can do to change it.

"If I have a bad game, they say it's because I'm just a dumb quarterback. If we have a good game, they say everybody else had a good game and Bradshaw was just out there."

Bradshaw's problems reached a climax a couple days before the game against Minnesota. "I went to the trouble of having lunch with a lady reporter and the first thing she asks me is, 'Terry, are you really that dumb?' I just walked away.

"People are funny," Bradshaw said. "If you talk slow, you're dumb. If you talk fast, you're a sharpie. If you dress one way, you're a hippie. Another way, you're a conservative. The heck with 'em. I know what I can do."

Bradshaw's teammate, Joe Greene, the leader of the defensive line, which was called the Steel Curtain, also had a problem with his image. The 270-pound defensive tackle was known as Mean Joe Greene.

"But I'm not mean," he said. "In college, I played at North Texas State. The school colors were green and the team was called the Mean Green. That's how I got my name, but now little kids are afraid to ask for my autograph."

Despite all this, the Steelers were the obvious favorites of most of the people in New Orleans and throughout the country. That was because of Art Rooney, Sr., the team's 75-year-old owner.

During the week of Super Bowl IX, Rooney was the most popular man in New Orleans. The kindly old guy beamed with pride at the work his sons, Dan and Art, Jr., had done in helping Noll make the team a contender.

Dan ran the day-to-day operation of the franchise and Art served as chief scout of college players, both having been around the club since they were youngsters.

The Steelers had been built through the college draft. Beginning with Joe Greene, the first player they chose when Noll became coach in 1969, the Steelers put together a team with 34 draft choices. Nine others had been signed as first-year free agents, three had come in trades, and one on waivers.

Of the last four, Mansfield was the only full-time player.

Unlike many Super Bowl teams of the past, the Steelers seemed to enjoy the attention and distractions of Super Bowl week. "I can't understand why guys complain about the press," said Mansfield. "For ten years, nobody ever knew who I was."

It was as if there was only one team in New Orleans. Although the Vikings were making their third appearance in five years in the Super Bowl, they were hardly noticed.

The Vikings were hardly noticeable during the game, either. As Miami had the last two Super

Bowls, the Steelers dominated Super Bowl IX.

The Steelers' defense was so much in control that Minnesota gained only 17 yards rushing, 12 fewer than Oakland had in the AFC championship game. Quarterback Fran Tarkenton completed only 11 of 27 passes for 102 yards. Three of his passes were intercepted, four were deflected by Steelers' defenders. Many were thrown under pressure.

It was the Steelers' defense which scored the game's first points. Tarkenton tried to hand the ball to Dave Osborn at the Vikings' 10-yard line midway through the second quarter, but Osborn fumbled and Tarkenton recovered in the Vikings' end zone, where he was tackled. Pittsburgh was credited with a safety, and two points.

At the half, the Steelers' offense hadn't scored, but it had outgained Minnesota 129 yards to 11 on the ground and 165–76 overall. In the second half, the Steelers went to work.

Franco Harris, who broke Larry Csonka's Super Bowl rushing records with 34 carries and 158 yards, picked up 97 yards in the second half. He also scored a touchdown.

Terry Brown of Minnesota fumbled the third-quarter kickoff. Pittsburgh's Marv Kellum recovered at the Vikings' 30, and the Steelers scored in four plays. Harris ran around left end for nine yards and a 9–0 lead.

Minnesota still wasn't doing anything offensively, but its defense scored a touchdown at the beginning of the fourth quarter.

Bobby Walden's punt from the 15-yard line was blocked by Matt Blair and recovered in the end zone by Terry Brown. But Fred Cox missed

Two vital Steelers, defensive tackle Joe Greene and quarterback Terry Bradshaw, congratulate each other on super season.

the point after touchdown.

There still were more than 10 minutes left, but the Steelers controlled the ball for more than seven minutes in a 12-play, 66-yard drive that ended with Bradshaw passing four yards to Larry Brown for a touchdown.

That gave the Steelers a 16–6 lead and ended the scoring. The crowd of 80,997 persons who looked on in 46-degree weather knew the Steelers had dominated the game more than the score indicated.

They outgained the Vikings 333–119 and had 17 first downs to 9. In gaining only 17 yards on the ground, the Vikings averaged less than a yard on each of their 21 rushing attempts.

Bradshaw completed 9 of 14 passes for 96 yards and one touchdown and ran five times for 33 yards. He was particularly effective in the Steelers' march to the clinching touchdown.

His pass to Brown was a tough, clutch play . . . hardly the work of a stupid person.

"I looked first to pass to the halfback—Rocky Bleier—or I could have run the ball, or passed it to Brown," he said. "It depended on what their cornerbacks did. If they came up, I was going to pass. If they laid back, I was going to run.

"They laid back, so I started to run, but I knew I couldn't run the ball in for a touchdown. It was third down. On fourth down we might have had to settle for a field goal. That would have made the score only 12–6, and with three and a half minutes left in the game they had time to score a touchdown and beat us.

"Larry Brown then made a smart move; he stopped after running toward the corner of the end zone, then started again. It made the middle linebacker commit himself, and I drilled the ball to Larry."

The victory was the most rewarding of Bradshaw's career, but his performance in Super Bowl IX was no better than it had been since he stepped into the huddle in New England and chewed out his teammates.

Bradshaw came of age that day in New England, and so did the Steelers.

In the last five games of the season, including the Super Bowl, Bradshaw completed 47 of 79 passes for 612 yards and eight touchdowns . . . and threw only two interceptions.

During that span, the Steelers outscored their opponents 120–53, outgained them 1,683–1,038, and out first-downed them 93–72.

Franco Harris,who was named the most valuable player of Super Bowl IX, gained 558 yards in 133 carries in the five-game stretch, scoring seven touchdowns.

Like Bradshaw and Greene, Harris was a number one draft choice. The Steelers selected him in 1972. He gained 1,000 yards rushing for the second time in his three seasons in 1974.

"Gaining one thousand yards is good," he said. "Contributing to winning a Super Bowl championship is even better. Since all of that happened this year, I would have to say this is the most significant year of my life."

Chuck Noll, the Steelers' coach, already had his eye on the future. "We'll probably only enjoy this victory a short time," he said. "Then we'll have to get back to preparing for next season."

The Steelers planned to take their place

alongside Green Bay and Miami in Super Bowl history by winning two straight. Only time would tell if they were to be successful.

```
PITTSBURGH. . . . . . . . .  0   2   7   7   —   16
MINNESOTA. . . . . . . . .   0   0   0   6   —    6
```

Pitt—Safety, White downed Tarkenton in end zone

Pitt—Harris 12 run (Gerela kick)

Minn—T. Brown recovered blocked punt in end zone (kick failed)

Pitt—L. Brown 4 pass from Bradshaw (Gerela kick)

Attendance—80,997

Reggie Harrison (46) goes high in the air to block Mitch Hoopes's punt. It gave the Steelers a safety and turned game around.

SUPER BOWL

The Super Play

The Pittsburgh Steelers call the play "60 Flanker Post."

Loosely translated, it means that three receivers, two less than the maximum number, go out for a pass. The flanker, who is the wide receiver on the side of the tight end, runs a pattern that takes him toward the goal posts.

That was the route Lynn Swann used to beat the Dallas Cowboys in Super Bowl X, the best of all the Super Bowls. It was the Super Bowl that had everything the first nine only had part of: Excitement, big plays, evenly-matched teams, and drama.

The Steelers won when Swann and quarterback Terry Bradshaw got together on a 64-yard touchdown play late in the fourth quarter. But it wasn't until the final play of the game that the Miami Orange Bowl crowd of 80,187 persons and a national television audience of more than 80 million uttered a sigh of relief, or an expletive of frustration.

That was after the Steelers' Glen Edwards

leaped high in the Pittsburgh end zone and intercepted a pass thrown by Dallas's Roger Staubach.

"Sixty-Nine Maximum Flanker Post" was the biggest play of Super Bowl X, but it was only one of many big plays.

It had been that kind of year for Swann, the Steelers, and the Cowboys.

Swann emerged in 1975 as one of the top pass-catchers in the NFL after being the Steelers' number one draft choice in 1974. Eleven of his 49 catches in 1975 went for touchdowns.

The development of Swann was just one of the reasons the Steelers were making their second consecutive trip to the Super Bowl.

After beating Minnesota in Super Bowl IX, Pittsburgh came back even stronger in 1975. Bradshaw played as well as he had in the final five games the year before—only this time he played well all season. Franco Harris was an even stronger runner, and the defense was over-powering.

The Steelers beat Baltimore 28–10 in the first round of the playoffs and they outlasted Oakland in 16-degree weather to win the AFC championship 16–10.

But the biggest difference, it seemed, was the attitude pro football fans had taken toward the Steelers the week of the Super Bowl. The Steelers had been the popular favorite at Super Bowl IX. They were the young team trying to establish itself against the Minnesota Vikings, who were playing in their third Super Bowl.

But it was just the opposite in Super Bowl X. The Cowboys had caught the public's fancy. For years, Dallas *had* represented the established order. It had qualified for the playoffs eight straight times from 1966 through 1973. It had been to the Super Bowl twice, losing in game V and winning in game VI.

But the Cowboys failed to make the playoffs in 1974. And they entered the 1975 season with 12 first-year players in what was described as a rebuilding program.

Dallas surprised itself by finishing second to St. Louis in the NFC East. The Cowboys gained the playoffs as a wild-card team with the best second-place record in the NFC. They beat Minnesota 17–14 in the first round of the playoffs when Drew Pearson caught Roger Staubach's long, desperation pass for a 50-yard touchdown with 24 seconds to play.

The Cowboys won the NFC championship the next week by overwhelming the favored Los Angeles Rams 37–7. Both victories came under the added burden of having to play on the road. Their own fans even doubted their chances of getting to the Super Bowl.

But when Dallas took a 21–0 lead in the second quarter at Los Angeles, airline ticket offices in Dallas were swamped with reservations for Miami.

Preston Pearson was one of the heroes of the Rams' game, scoring three touchdowns. Pearson and linebacker Warren Capone were the only players on the team who were not originally signed by Dallas.

Pearson had played five seasons with Pittsburgh. The Steelers released him at the final cutdown in September. No team claimed Pear-

Drew Pearson scored on a 29-yard pass from Roger Staubach to give the Cowboys a 7-0 lead in the first quarter.

son on waivers. A couple days later the Cowboys signed him as a free agent.

From the beginning of Super Bowl X, it was apparent that the Steelers and Cowboys weren't friendly rivals. Both teams took it to the other with hard blocking and solid tackling.

Dallas scored first in the first quarter on a 29-yard pass from Staubach to Drew Pearson. This happened on the play following a fumbled snap from center by Pittsburgh's Bobby Walden, who was tackled by Billy Joe DuPree after recovering the ball.

The Steelers quickly tied the score, however, when Bradshaw passed seven yards to Randy Grossman. That play ended an eight-play drive that began on the Steelers' 33. Swann's diving catch of a 32-yard Bradshaw pass kept the drive alive.

Dallas's Tony Fritsch kicked a 36-yard field goal in the second quarter and the Cowboys hung on to a 10–7 lead for the next 33 minutes of play.

The momentum was with Dallas for most of the afternoon, but it changed three minutes into the fourth quarter. The Cowboys' Mitch Hoopes was attempting a punt from his 15-yard line, but Reggie Harrison, a reserve running back and special teams player for Pittsburgh, burst through to block the kick.

The ball rocketed out of the Dallas end zone and the Steelers had a safety and two points. Dallas also had to give up possession and kick to the Steelers again.

Mike Collier returned Hoopes' next try 25 yards to the Cowboys' 45-yard line. The Steelers marched to the 20 in seven plays before Roy Gerela kicked a 36-yard field goal.

Now the score was 12–10 in favor of Pittsburgh.

Harrison wasn't aware of the chain of events he had started.

"I was yelling and screaming," he said. "When I went back to the bench after the safety I didn't realize we got any points. Next thing I remembered we were lining up to kick off after the field goal. We were ahead by two points."

Harrison asked teammate Jim Allen what happened. "You turned the game around," said Allen.

"When it happened, we were behind and I was worried," Harrison said later. "All I thought about was we were behind."

"We knew they were coming," said Hoopes. "You could see it; that didn't bother us. But I don't know what happened. I was concentrating on the ball and all of a sudden, I saw this flash out of the corner of my eye. I knew then it was going to be blocked. I knew then I should have kicked it sooner."

The Steelers weren't through. Mike Wagner intercepted a pass from Staubach to Drew Pearson on the first play after the field goal and returned it 19 yards to Dallas's 7.

The Cowboys' defense held, but Gerela kicked an 18-yard field goal for a 15–10 lead with a little more than nine minutes left.

Once again the Cowboys could do nothing with the ball and punted. Pittsburgh took over on its 30 with 4:25 to go.

On the first play, Franco Harris ran up the

middle four yards. Harris then gained two yards at right tackle. Now it was third down and six yards to go for a first down. There were slightly more than three minutes left in the game.

The big play of the game, and the season, was next.

Bradshaw called "69 Maximum Flanker Post" in the huddle.

Bradshaw took the ball from center and began back pedaling almost in one motion. Steelers' pass receivers flew out in all directions. The Dallas defense was coming.

Cliff Harris blitzed from his free safety position and delivered a jolting blow to the side of Bradshaw's helmet, a fraction of a second after Bradshaw arched a long, high pass down the middle of the field.

Cowboys' cornerback Mark Washington matched Swann stride for stride, but at the last second Swann got a step on the defender and hauled in Bradshaw's pass over his left shoulder.

Swann broke Washington's tackle at the 5-yard line and eased into the end zone. The ball was thrown 59 yards. It was the most important catch of Swann's pro career and the biggest completion Bradshaw ever had made.

But Bradshaw was not aware of what happened—not until the game was over. He had to be helped to the dressing room for treatment of a concussion suffered when he was hit by Harris.

Swann had suffered a concussion in the AFC championship game. He was carried from the field unconscious in that game and there was some doubt he would be able to play in Super Bowl X. Swann had a miserable week of practice

Before his touchdown catch in the fourth quarter, Swann caught a pass over Mark Washington to set up Steelers' first touchdown.

before the game.

"I was worried that my timing and concentration were off," said Swann, whose four catches for 161 yards set a Super Bowl record. He was named the game's most valuable player.

"But I told myself, 'Hey, this is it. Either play your best or not at all.' I couldn't have played a week ago. But I felt all right yesterday, so I thought I'd be all right for the game."

Swann had an added reason for wanting to play. "During the week I read an article where Cliff Harris was talking about how he was known as a hitter and how I had to be thinking about my concussion and how I would be scared coming across the middle of the field on a pass pattern."

Harris tried to remind Swann early in the game. Swann caught a 53-yard pass from Bradshaw and on the next play Harris came up and said, "Boy, you're lucky I wasn't heading your way or I would have belted you and put you out of the game."

"I told him, 'If you come at me, I'm liable to put *you* out of the game.' Obviously, Cliff Harris does not know me, or the Pittsburgh Steelers."

The Bradshaw-to-Swann touchdown seemingly locked up the victory, but Dallas wasn't through. The Cowboys took the kickoff and drove 80 yards. Staubach's 34-yard pass to Percy Howard made the score 21–17 with 1:56 left.

Pittsburgh coach Chuck Noll then took a big gamble.

The Steelers recovered Tony Fritsch's attempted onside kickoff at Dallas's 42 with 1:47 remaining. But two carries by Harris and one by

Rocky Bleier gained only one yard. Dallas used its time outs after each play, so 1:33 still remained.

The situation normally called for the Steelers to punt the ball and push Dallas deep into its own territory. But Noll was worried about the possibility that the Cowboys might block a punt.

Noll elected not to punt. Bleier carried for one yard on fourth down and Dallas took over on its 39 with 1:22 remaining. Two plays later the Cowboys were on Pittsburgh's 38 and almost a minute of play was left. But Staubach's next two passes were incomplete and his third was intercepted by Edwards as the game ended.

"The Cowboys' rush was too strong," said Noll. "If they had blocked the punt, the ball might have rolled halfway to our end zone. I told [Terry] Hanratty [who had replaced Bradshaw] to hand off to Rocky, get what yardage he could, then let our defense do the rest.

"Field position was not a factor," said Noll. "The difference between Dallas having to go eighty yards or sixty yards isn't that much when they need a touchdown and have to pass. If they'd only needed a field goal, we'd have punted. We decided to rely on one of our strengths: our defense."

"What Chuck did was beautiful," said Steelers' defensive end L.C. Greenwood. "He turned the game over to us in the final minute. The whole darn season, everything we worked for since July, was on the line and he left it up to us. We wouldn't have wanted it any other way."

Not all of the Steelers felt that way. "I didn't know what Chuck's thinking was on that," said

Bleier. "When Hanratty called my number, I thought, 'Well, I'm not the biggest back, or the fastest. . . .'"

"I think maybe it would have been better to punt," said center Roy Mansfield. "But what the heck, we won."

Dallas coach Tom Landry was more concerned with what happened when the Cowboys' punt was blocked earlier in the game. "That changed the momentum," he said. "It cost us five points . . . a safety and a field goal. We lost twenty-one to seventeen. Those five points were the difference."

After the game, four young Steelers' fans were walking toward the parking lot.

"Super Bowl nine. . . mighty fine,"one of them hummed.

"Super Bowl ten . . . did it again," sang the other.

```
DALLAS............. 7  3  0  7  — 17
PITTSBURGH........ 7  0  0  14 — 21
Dal—D. Pearson 29 pass from Staubach
(Fritsch kick)
Pitt—Grossman 7 pass from Bradshaw
(Gerela kick)
Dal—FG Fritsch 36
Pitt—Safety, Harrison blocked kick out of end
zone
Pitt—FG Gerela 36
Pitt—FG Gerela 18
Pitt—Swann 64 pass from Bradshaw (kick
failed)
Dal—P. Howard 34 pass from Staubach
(Fritsch kick)
Attendance—80,187
```

Super Bowl Records

INDIVIDUAL

SERVICE

Most Games
- 5   Marv Fleming, Green Bay, I & II, Miami, VI, VII, & VIII
- 4   Herb Adderley, Green Bay, I & II, Dallas, V & VI; Earl Morrall, Baltimore, III & V, Miami, VII & VIII

SCORING

Most Points, Career
- 20   Don Chandler, Green Bay, I & II
- 13   Mike Clark, Dallas, V & VI

Most Points, Game
- 15   Don Chandler, Green Bay, II

Most Touchdowns, Game
- 2   Max McGee, Green Bay, I; Elijah Pitts, Green Bay, I; Bill Miller, Oakland, II; Larry Csonka, Miami VIII

Most Field Goals, Game
- 4   Don Chandler, Green Bay, II

Longest Field Goal
- 48   Jan Stenerud, Kansas City, IV

BALL CARRYING

Most Attempts, Career
- 61   Franco Harris, Pittsburgh, IX & X
- 57   Larry Csonka, Miami, VI, VII, & VIII

Most Attempts, Game
- 34   Franco Harris, Pittsburgh, IX

Most Yards Gained, Career
- 297   Larry Csonka, Miami, VI, VII, & VIII
- 240   Franco Harris, Pittsburgh, IX & X

Most Yards Gained, Game
- 158   Franco Harris, Pittsburgh, IX

Longest Gain
- 58   Tom Matte, Baltimore, III

PASSING

Most Attempts, Career
- 54   Fran Tarkenton, Minnesota, VIII & IX
- 47   Bart Starr, Green Bay, I & II

Most Attempts, Game
- 34   Daryle Lamonica, Oakland, II

Most Completions, Career
- 29   Bart Starr, Green Bay, I & II
-      Fran Tarkenton, Minnesota, VIII & IX

Most Yards Gained, Career
   452 Bart Starr, Green Bay, I & II
   353 Len Dawson, Kansas City, I & IV

Most Yards Gained, Game
   250 Bart Starr, Green Bay, I

Longest Completion
   75   John Unitas (to Mackey), Baltimore V (touchdown)

Most Touchdowns, Game
   2   Bart Starr, Green Bay, I
        Daryle Lamonica, Oakland, II
        Roger Staubach, Dallas, VI & X
        Terry Bradshaw, Pittsburgh, X

PASS RECEIVING

Most Receptions, Career
   10   Otis Taylor, Kansas City, I & IV
        Chuck Foreman, Minnesota, VIII & IX

Most Receptions, Game
   8   George Sauer, New York Jets, III

Most Yards Gained, Career
   173 Max McGee, Green Bay, I & II
   161 Lynn Swann, Pittsburgh, IX & X

Most Yards Gained, Game
   161 Lynn Swann, Pittsburgh, X

INTERCEPTIONS

Most Interceptions By, Career
   3   Chuck Howley, Dallas, V & VI
   2   Randy Beverly, New York Jets, III
        Jake Scott, Miami, VI, VII, & VIII
        Mike Wagner, Pittsburgh, IX & X

Most Interceptions by, Game
   2   Randy Beverly, New York Jets, III
        Chuck Howley, Dallas, V
        Jake Scott, Miami, VII

Longest Return
   60   Herb Adderley, Green Bay, II (touchdown)

PUNTING

Longest Punt
   61   Jerrel Wilson, Kansas City, I

Highest Punting Average, Game
   48.5 Jerrel Wilson, Kansas City, IV (4 punts)

PUNT RETURNS

Most Punt Returns, Game
   5   Willie Wood, Green Bay, II

Most Yards Gained, Game
   35   Willie Wood, Green Bay, II

Longest Punt Return, Game

   31   Willie Wood, Green Bay, II

Highest Average, Game

  11.3 Lynn Swann, Pittsburgh, IX (3 returns)

KICKOFF RETURNS

Most Yards Gained, Game

   90   Jim Duncan, Baltimore, V

Longest Return

   48   Thomas Henderson, Dallas, X

Highest Average, Game

  22.5 Jim Duncan, Baltimore, V (4 returns)
          Mercury Morris, Miami, VI (4 returns)

TEAM
SCORING

Most Points, Game

   35   Green Bay, I

Fewest Points, Game

    3   Miami, VI

Most Points, Both Teams, Game

   47   Green Bay (33) vs. Oakland (14), II

Fewest Points, Both Teams, Game

   21   Washington (7) vs. Miami (14), VII

FIRST DOWNS

Most First Downs, Game

   23   Dallas, VI

Fewest First Downs, Game

    9   Minnesota, IX

NET YARDS GAINED

Most Yards Gained, Game

  358 Green Bay, I

Fewest Yards Gained, Game

  119 Minnesota, IX

Most Yards Gained, Both Teams, Game

  661 New York Jets (337) vs. Baltimore (324), III

Fewest Yards Gained, Both Teams, Game

  452 Minnesota (119) vs. Pittsburgh (333), IX